OVERANALYZE

Lauren Hope Bartling

Book Cover by Kristina Conatser, CapturedbyKCDesigns.com
Edited by Dragonfly De La Luz, DragonflyEditing.com
Book Design by James Woosley, FreeAgentPress.com

ISBN: 979-8-9930701-0-0 (hardcover)
ISBN: 979-8-9930701-1-7 (paperback)
ISBN: 979-8-9930701-2-4 (ebook)

For My Mom

Without your love and support, I wouldn't be here today. Thank you for always believing in me and my dreams. You've been my biggest cheerleader since day one, and I'm so blessed to have you as my mother and my best friend. Here's the book we've both been waiting for.

"Write hard and clear about what hurts."

— *Ernest Hemingway*

AUTHOR'S NOTE

Hi, I'm Lauren Hope Bartling, and I am honored to introduce you to my first poetry book, *Overanalyze.*

I am a writer, poet, storyteller, dreamer, and over-thinker. I started writing as a hobby in high school amid deep depression as a means to cope and release the emotions I had been repressing. Many of the poems are from that dark time and subsequent seasons of depression and low points in my life. For anyone in a similar place, I want you to know that I've been there. I know what it's like. Please know that things will get better. It is okay if you need help; don't be afraid to reach out for support or treatment. You may be hurting today, but I assure you, you will not always feel this way. If you are looking for a sign to persevere, this is it.

Overanalyze is a collection of poetry, prose, short stories, and personal essays that I've been writing and compiling since I was in high school.

To me, connection is one of the greatest gifts we can give one another; it's the reason we exist. Because of this, I greatly value transparency and honesty. I am very open, often to a fault, about the hardships I've faced in my life. I believe that it's important to talk about the things we've been through. Your story has the potential to help someone else in ways you may not even know. I know this because hearing others' stories has helped me find the courage to share mine, and I hope my story inspires the same.

I believe poetry to be a safe haven for the exploration of human emotion. We exist to create and consume art. To love. To feel. And everything I do, I do deeply, wholeheartedly.

Overanalyze is largely reflective of my struggles with mental health and an expression of my predisposition to overthink. I have complex post-traumatic stress disorder (C-PTSD), generalized anxiety disorder (GAD), panic disorder, and depression. Over the years of acquiring these diagnoses and learning how to cope with them, I've found writing to be therapeutic for me; it's my sanctuary. Because I try not to censor my emotions whilst writing, many of these pieces revolve around heavy topics such as childhood trauma, mental illness, abuse, self-harm, and suicide. I understand the gravity of these subjects and how they can be overwhelming to read about, so please proceed with caution.

However, it must be said that not every piece in this book is categorically "sad," although many people may categorize my writing as such. In this book, I've also included poems about people I've known, people I've loved, and people I've lost. I like to think of these pieces as love letters that were left unsent, or perhaps letters in general — letters of rage, confusion, sadness, adoration, or infatuation. *Overanalyze* can be summarized by the ideas of youthful reminiscing, both happy and sad. I hope you find something that resonates with you.

This book is a piece of my heart in the form of writing, so please be gentle with it.

All my love,

Lauren Hope Bartling

TO YOU, FROM ME

This is a book for:
The lovers
The wishers
The wanters
The criers
The hopers
The fighters
The survivors
The triers
And the people who inspire people like me —
The writers.

WILL I EVER LEARN?

10/18/18
1:20 pm

The hardest thing I've ever done
was learn how to forgive my father.
And I'm still learning.

ODIUM

I hate you.
You have broken me apart.
You have made me doubt my sanity.
You have made me question my abilities.
You have caused me nightmares
and so many tears.

Because of you, I've been filled with fear.
It's been instilled in me from a young age.

The fear of never being loved,
because you never loved me.
The fear of never being good enough,
because I was never good enough for you.
The fear of failure,
because you never believed in me.
The fear of trusting others,
because you were untrustworthy.
The fear of alcohol and drugs,
because you showed me what addiction means.
The fear of never being loved by a man,
because you were supposed to be the first man to love me.

You were supposed to show me
how a man should treat me, instead,
you've shown me how a man shouldn't.

I can't watch a movie with a profound
father-daughter bond without crying,
because I will never be able to relate
to what that kind of love feels like.
I've missed out on such an important part of my life
all because you felt it was my responsibility
to develop a relationship with you.

The adult in this scenario
with a sense of duty
was never meant to be me.

And I shouldn't have to beg you for a relationship
when you are the reason we don't have one.
You are the reason I cannot trust others.
You are the reason that I feel I am not worthy of love.
You are the reason I have low self-esteem.
You are the reason I assume
all the fruits of my labor
will amount to nothing,
because you told me as a child
that dreams don't come true,
and *I believed you.*

It's no wonder that I don't feel good enough,
because you made me feel like I'm not.
Was I not enough for you to want to talk to me?
To get to know me?
To care about me?
To love me?

Loving goes beyond words,
but that's all you could muster.

Never any action or evidence,
only mere sentences spoken on occasion.
Love is active, but you were always passive.

I will never get the one thing I've always wanted,
the one thing I feel entitled to have,
the one thing I feel is owed to me.
And in that lacking, I feel so much suffering,
so much anguish and fury.
Lovelorn over someone who was meant to adore me.

I'm lovesick and furious.
And it's such a pity —
you had all the tools to be a good man,
but you never used them.
I bought you instruction manuals that lay untouched,
and still, you told me I was to blame
for the faulty construction of our frame.
It was a cracked foundation you laid.
It's your penance to be paid, not mine.

I wear this pain like a necklace,
a tattoo,
an embroidered symbol of you.
Your initials in big bold print,
the ache in my heart with your name stitched across it.

And you will miss out on the pleasure of knowing me,
And I feel so sorry, *for you and me,*
but for differing reasons.

Reasons that you can't see.

OPHTHALMOLOGY

I'm sorry you couldn't see
all the ways you hurt me,
so I wrote this book to show you,
unapologetically.

Maybe now you can see
a little more clearly
and you'll realize
just how much you've hurt me.

You were never more than
just a physically present
absentee parent to me.

WILL I EVER GET OVER YOU?

How much must I write about you
before I feel better?
Will I ever feel better?
The thought hits me in my stomach,
the fear that I'll never be rid of you.

I feel like a part of me is missing,
absent and aching.
A hollow space that sits
in the cavity of my chest.
A space you were meant to fill.
I'm a puzzle with a piece missing,
so I'm left incomplete.

A girl without a father,
in theory.
Because you were present,
you were there,
I'll give you that much.
But you weren't what I needed.

Presence doesn't equate to anything
when your absence leaves a tangible sting.
Physically present but emotionally distant,
I still blame myself for my heart's resistance.

I tell myself that I'm okay,
that I didn't need you,
despite the ever-present truth that I did,
and I do.
I tell myself that I made it this far without you.
But my heart still hurts,
and the hems I've sewn in my heart,
where you tore it apart,
aren't as strong as they ought to be.

Sewn together by a child's hands
and held together with hope.
And when the seams come undone,
I'm left with reminders of what you've done,
and why I can't trust you,
despite my desire to.

And for some twisted reason,
I feel the need to apologize on your behalf.
To apologize for me,
and who I am,
and all that I couldn't be.
In your eyes, I was always insufficient,
always lacking.
I'm sorry I wasn't a good enough daughter,
but you never apologized for being an awful father,
never with sincerity,
or integrity,
never acknowledging your wrongdoings.
And since I know you'll never apologize,
I'll say sorry on your behalf.
And I'll say all the things you never could.

I'll be a better man than you ever could've been.
I'll say the phrase
I'll never get to hear you say.

And I'll find someone
who doesn't deem it a chore
to get to know me.
I'll find someone
who says it's easy to love me.
I'll find someone
who will take the time
to bond with me.

And I realize
I shouldn't apologize
for my father being uninterested in me.

But one of us has to apologize,
and we both know it won't be you.
So I'll apologize for existing and breathing,
and I'll spend every day aching and reeling,
feeling inadequate and angry
for how you made me.
I'll apologize for who I am,
and I'll feel guilty for taking up space,
and I'll hurt myself
because I feel deserving of pain.

And once you're gone
my pain will be self-inflicted,
because you taught me to live was to ache,
so I assume I deserve suffering.

And I try to convince myself
of the truth,
that your words held no weight,
no truth,
but I find it hard to persuade my rotten brain.
And deep down I know how wonderful I am,
and I've watched the tragedy unfold before me,
of your life and your legacy.
And I feel sorry
for all that you've missed out on,
by not knowing me.

The truth is,
I may never feel better.
The hole in my heart might never shrink.
There's a large possibility
that it's a permanent part of me.
The hollow space you've carved,
an everlasting scar on my heart
that will never heal;
a wound that won't close.

To this day I have a distrust of men
because you never proved to me
that men were trustworthy.
You never showed me
that I was worthy of love.
And if how you treated me
was a reflection of love
it's not something I find myself fond of.

Because I'm not sure what's worse,
convincing myself that you truly loved me,
or settling on the idea
that you could never love another.
Perhaps that might make me feel less woeful,
knowing that I wasn't the defective one.

You had a God-complex,
thinking you were better than everyone else.
You looked outward
and into a crowd,
in church pews
and crowded bars,
and you dared to feel *superiority*.
I'll never get that mentality,
because when I look out into a sea of people
all I feel is *inferiority*,
a trait that I attribute to my upbringing.
As a child, I was always second-best,
runner-up, never a star student,
never the apple of your eye.

You'd call me your princess
but you never treated me like one.
You said the right things,
you knew what to do,
who to be,
but you never took
the initiative to follow through.

Always playing pretend,
putting on a show,
but never anything real,
nothing substantial.
All for looks,
playing the part assigned to you,
but never behind closed doors,
only for the public to see.

And I still ache.

Your name still hurts when I say it,
and the memory of you is like a knife
carving away at my insides.

This pain may persist forever,
but I've grown accustomed to it.

So I persist,
not because of,
but despite you.

A DREAMER WHO NEVER
HAD THE CHANCE TO DREAM

"Dreams don't come true"
was yelled at me
far too young
and way too soon.

I was taught to see my dreams
crushed
    right
        before
            my very eyes.

You never had the right to tell me that,
especially after you facilitated my dreams.
Just because our dreams differed

doesn't make mine any less valid.
Just because you couldn't be successful
doesn't mean I won't be.

But because of those words
I've been stuck in the mindset
that I shouldn't even try,
because of the possibility
of failure,
which you made me believe was inevitable.

So why bother, why try,
when it'll amount to nothing in the end?

I'm so afraid of failure,
I won't try.
I'll only ever be mediocre,
that's what you've convinced me.
You made me doubt myself
and my abilities.
So I'll do what everyone else does,
fit in with the crowd and follow the American dream,
because mine was just too "silly."

So I hope you're happy
knowing I'll never be.
I hope you can live out
all your wildest dreams
that I was never able to
because of those four words you said to me.

Why did you say it?
And why did you say it with such cruelty?
No remorse or reasoning,
just harsh words that left a mark on me.
Were you trying to hurt me
or make yourself feel better?
Or even worse, *both?*

I hope you're happy knowing you broke me
and shattered my dreams
before I could ever dream them up.

I've become an adult with no compass,
no goals,
afraid to dream,
afraid to hope.
I'll never shake the feeling of inadequacy.
I was so young,
so I believed what you said,
blindly.
I trusted you,
because I was supposed to.
So I told my friends
that their dreams were foolish.
I convinced myself
that my childhood dream
was an impossibility.

The opportunities I missed
because of what you said to me
were plenty,
and the dreams I have left
are few.
But over the years
I've convinced myself
that what you said to me so long ago
wasn't true.
At least I've tried to.

I still fear failure,
but I've chosen to dream,
despite what you said to me.

But I'll never forget
those words,
and it's too late for you to undo the damage.

Because of you,
I'm afraid if I speak I will stutter,
so I write.
I write because of you
and *in spite of you.*
I only feel confident when I'm writing,
where I can unburden my heart
without judgment,
where I make sense of it all.
But I struggle to believe
that anyone would ever purchase my writing.
And it's all because of you.
It always boils back down to you.
Y O U.
You are the reason
for my ache
and my doubts,
but you'd never say
that you let me down.

I hoped one day you'd read this
and know how deeply you've hurt me,
but it's too late for redemption.
You'll never get to see
the damage you've done
and the ways you've traumatized me.
You never cared about me,
not truly.

You never believed in me,
and even if you did,
you never would've said it.
You were meant to build me up,
but all you did was tear me down.
You hated that I didn't do what you wanted.
You expected me to be a puppet on your strings.
I made my own path, and you despised me for that.

I've spent hours
yelling and screaming,
begging to be heard.
Trying to get you to see
how you hurt me,
but no amount of words
could make you see clearly.
Perhaps that's why I write
so incessantly,
always with the hope
that you'd finally hear me.
You always claimed to be faultless,
saying you never hurt me
despite me telling you
that you had.

I know I'm not meant to hold grudges,
but I find it comes naturally.
It's a cozy embrace
like a baby blanket,
some kindling
to the fire you started in me.

I hold a grudge like a trophy.

My rage runs deep,
but just below the surface
lies a profound sadness,
an ache that never ceases.
A primal part of me is so broken,
innately scarred and ruined,
all thanks to you.
Y O U.

You were meant to love me the most;
you loved me the least.
I don't know what I did
to become so undeserving
of a father's love,
and I'll never understand
why you simply gave up.

Even now I'm unsure of what to call you.
Calling you dad seems too informal.
Father doesn't seem well suited.
So I've been calling you
by your name
for years.
Not that you were ever around to hear.
You don't deserve
the title of "father"
or "dad"
so I call you by your legal name,
and I leave it at that.

I want to hate you.
And I think a part of me does.
But another part of me
wanted to hold onto the hope
that maybe one day you would care.
But you never did, not even on your deathbed.
You said the words,
you played the part,
but that's all you did.

"I love you"
never sounded more disingenuous
than when it came from you.
You can't do the things you did to me
and call it love.
That wasn't love, *that was agony.*
That was anguish and suffering.
Now all I am is malice and confusion.
Guilt and nothing.
I am numb to the sting of losing you.

Because
you
first
lost me.

I had hoped that maybe one day
you'd care enough about me
to exchange more than a handful of words a day.

"Good morning."
"How was your day?"
"Goodnight."
And the insincere "I love you"
that you'd say as I walked up the stairs
to my bedroom each night.
Ten words on any given day
that you never actually
cared to hear a response to.
You'd ask me how I was,
but it was a thoughtless ask.
That was all I ever heard from you
unless you were talking about yourself.

You never bothered to ask me
about my life or my interests.
You never even bothered to get to know me,
your own daughter,
your flesh and blood.
You didn't know my teachers' names,
my friends' names,
my favorite subjects.
You didn't know
the most basic traits about me.
How awful is that?
Who could do that?
It's not a million-dollar question,
but the answer is you.
It's always you.
You.

You're the reason I'm so messed up.
A perfect recipe for mental illness:
childhood trauma and a deadbeat dad.
It's almost textbook,
the kind of narcissistic jerk you were.

Even one of my therapists called you a "fucking asshole"
and cried
when I talked about you.
So nobody could convince me
that you were a good man,
when I saw who you truly were *firsthand.*

I had to go to therapy because of you,
but you didn't even care,
you never even knew.
You didn't bother to research
my mental illnesses
that were caused by you.
And I don't want to blame you,
but there's nobody else to.
It's your fault at the end of the day,
and you can't keep pinning it on me.
I wanted you to change so desperately,
but holding out hope for you
became painful for me.

Every time I'd hope,
I would only get let down,
time and time again,
a vicious cycle of disappointment.

I'm livid
because it's unfair
that you didn't have to suffer
the consequences of your misdeeds,
the ways that you failed me.

I wasn't allowed to dream
while you were here,
but we've been apart for years,
so I'm permitting myself
to pursue my dreams wholeheartedly.
I'm following my dreams
despite what you said to me.
I'll make a name for myself,
one that isn't attached to you.

It makes me sad you didn't live to see
the dreams you told me were improbable
falling into place
    right
        before
           me.

A Note for Parents:

What you say matters. What you tell your kids is important. This one statement that my dad spoke to me changed me forever, and not for the better. The way you speak to your child matters. The words you say to them will have everlasting consequences. So choose your words wisely, and please tell your children you love them. And more than that, show them that you love them. Get to know them — truly know them — and make sure they know you care. That's all kids want — someone who cares. Show an interest in their lives and who they are. You have the honor and privilege of parenthood; don't take it for granted. Your child is a unique person with unique traits and interests. You don't have to be perfect; you just have to be present. Make an effort to be in their lives and make sure your kids know they are enough. Ensure your children know how deeply they are loved.

THE SHAPING

You hurt me,
and you don't
get to say that
you didn't.
Because you did.
You hurt me.
Endlessly.
Without apology.

SOMEWHERE IN-BETWEEN

You speak
and all I want to do is scream.
I clench my jaw and tighten my hands into fists,
trying so hard not to punch the wall
like I've done many times before,
making my knuckles bleed and bruise,
taking my anger out on non-living things
so the only thing that gets hurt is me.
And it's fine,
because I feel deserving.
So I self-inflict pain,
because I am a child
who was spoon-fed so much poison,
I consider *harm* a *comfort*.
You belittle me and it takes everything
in me to simply nod back
without speaking,
knowing if I were to speak
it would only make things worse.
It only ever made things worse.
You leave after breaking my heart once again.
You aren't good at much,
but you were always good
at *leaving* instead of *loving*.
I guess that was your specialty,
because you never learned how to love me,
and I'm not sure I wanted you to,
because being loved by someone like you
would make me just as culpable as you.
You convinced me I was to blame.

The idea was ingrained
in me from a tender age
that I ruined everything I touched —
the antithesis of a Midas touch.
You convinced me I was poisonous.
I know the saying goes,
sticks and stones may break my bones —
but your words always hurt me.
You never bruised me,
but you tore me apart
with your words and actions
or lack thereof.
You spoke but never listened.
I don't think you ever wanted to.
The tears in my eyes blurred,
but my vision couldn't blind me
to who you truly were —
a sad excuse for a man,
insecure and jealous,
and you wanted others to be just as miserable as you.
You could never love another,
because the love you had for yourself
took up what little space you held in your heart.
I want to say I love you
but I can't,
because that would be a lie.
I neither hate you nor love you;
I'm somewhere in-between.
I cannot say *either* definitively,
because one would negate the other.
Yet somehow, both remain true.
I hate you.
And... I love you.

BRUISES

12/20/17
7:48 pm

My hand turned black and blue
from punching a wall,
wishing it was you.

WHERE WERE YOU?

6/2/18
6:25 pm

Father.
A person I've never known.
I had a dad,
but he was never a father to me.
Just another man
who disappointed me.

Nothing new,
simply something I'd grown used to.
How can someone
who only cares about himself
ever love me,
and how could I expect him to?

He spent more time
admiring his reflection
than he ever spent admiring me.
What good he saw?
I can't say I'll ever see.

We only ever shared conversations
about unimportant small talk.
And still, you always found a way
to bring the conversation back to you.
It might've been the only talent you had.
Compassion and empathy
weren't words in your vocabulary.

You couldn't go a day
without creating needless drama.

The arguments you initiated
were normal occurrences
I'm not sure what about it you enjoyed,
and I try not to sit and think about it.
Pondering the reason
you found enjoyment in others' suffering
is something I'll never want to understand.

I think some sick part of you wanted control
more than anything else,
so you made others feel small,
unworthy,
so they'd never leave you.
I dissipated into thin air around you,
slipping away mentally
before I ever had the chance to escape.

And, as it turns out,
when others don't play by your rules,
you rig the game.
I didn't abide by your orders,
so you left me
before I ever had the chance to leave.

Because even in your presence,
your absence was palpable.

Did you like seeing other people in pain?
Do you do it because you've been hurt,
so you want others to hurt like you have?

Or even worse, do you do it
just because that's all you know how to do?

I hate that I'm related to you.
And I hate that I've spent
so many hours crying over you
when you've never shed a tear over me.
I've spent so much of my life
feeling sorry for myself
for something I can't help,
a part of my history I can't change.

I will no longer
cut off pieces of myself and hope
that they'll be enough for you.
I'm done tearing myself
apart at the seams
trying to get you to love me.
I cannot make someone
who isn't capable of love,
love me.

I've tried
and I've tried
and now I can't anymore.
Loving you has become a tumultuous chore.
I left the ball in your court
and it sat for years,
deflating,
decaying.

You've scarred me,
permanently, irrevocably.

You tore me apart
trying to fix yourself.
Tell me, *did it help?*
You can't find salvation
at the bottom of a glass,
but that didn't stop you
from looking for it there.

I hope that one day
you might change.
So I wait
and hope you become
better than you've been.
But I fall asleep each night
knowing *that may never happen.*

So until that day comes,
I'm done.
I'm done fighting
for something we never had.
I'm done
getting my hopes up
only to be disappointed
once again.

Hopefully one day
you will change your ways
and realize your mistakes.
And hopefully, *it won't be too late.*

Spoiler Alert:
That day never came.

ABOUT MY FATHER

12/6/16
7:42 pm

Trying to reason with you
is like walking on a treadmill.
I think I'm making progress
and resolving our issues,
then I look down
and see my feet moving,
but my body is stationary.
I'm just walking in place,
with a false sense of hope
that I was getting somewhere,
when in reality...
I wasn't.

Now I run and sprint and leap.
Freely,
flowing,
away from you.
I see the earth moving below my feet.
I see the trees swaying above me,
blurring off in the distance.
I feel the heat of the pavement
radiating onto my body,
all because I let go
and gave up,
because I knew when it was time to.

I know what independence looks like,
and I'd never go back to your grasp
now that I've tasted
revolution.
That feeling of letting go
and realizing you can't change
things out of your control
is liberating
beyond anything I've ever known.

I'm still waiting for that day
where I look down and my feet are running,
not on artificial roads,
but on solid pavement,
trails of the earth.
I await the ability to run
far away from you,
to feel happy and free,
to gain back who I am.

And when that day comes,
I won't even think about the treadmill
I used to run on to try and fail to get to you.

ABOUT MY FATHER II

12/6/16
7:56 pm

I've been punched down
one too many times,
not physically
but emotionally.
A person can cause unseen scars
and have the audacity
to tell you
they never hurt you.
They'll make you feel
like you're the problem,
gaslighting you into submission,
making you think you're crazy
by denying the things
you know they did.
They love to point out every flaw,
depicting each fault with *excruciating detail.*
They will tear you down piece by piece,
then pretend they're the ones bleeding.
They will never admit to any fault
because they don't think they have any.
But it's not your fault.
You've bled
and you've cried
and you've suffered,
but you survived.
You made it through.
You didn't imagine it.

You aren't crazy,
despite what they may say.
Sure, you have flaws —
we all do.
But your imperfections don't define you.
And the people who cannot love you
do not determine your lovability.
You are worthy
and so easy to love,
despite those who didn't show you so.
You may be torn and jaded —
so am I.
But your garden will flourish again
and sprout new blooms
that will grow higher
than the ones before.

LEMONADE MOUTH

People tend to find comfort
in the arms of others;
you found comfort in a bottle.
You found fulfillment
at the bottom of a wine glass,
peace at the last drop of beer.
I poured out my heart
like you poured liquor —
endlessly.
You chose to listen
to your cold, numb heart
instead of the people who cared about you.
You broke me,
over and over,
and never seemed to notice.
Your grasp on the bottle
was too tight for anyone to loosen.

I was just a kid when I first noticed
something different in you.
Now I know the name for it:
addiction.
As I grew, I saw it more often,
your drunken state.
Always analyzing the shape you were in
when you came home each day...
I confronted you with tears in my eyes
blurring the sight of your intoxicated face,
while *Lemonade Mouth* played on the TV behind.

I screamed at you,
not understanding why.
I still don't.
I don't think I ever will.
The pain and suffering
caused by your hands
is unrelenting.
And as far as I'm concerned,
you're unforgiven.

The saddest part about this story
is the fact that I know you
won't change.
You can't,
not for me,
not for anyone —
not even yourself.

So you never did.
You never became a better man.

SCARCE, BUT DETRIMENTAL

10/19/18
10:07 am

Words.
Few they take
to make a heart break.

ARMCHAIR CONVERSATIONS

10/30/18
11:31 pm

I've cried too many tears over you,
wasted too many sleepless nights
worrying about you.
My once vivid dreams replaced
with nightmares of you.
I'm done
blaming myself
for all the things you did
and didn't do.
The fault lies solely with you.
I will no longer
let you dictate my emotions
the way you have done before.
It's time to settle the score.

So I'm forgiving you
for all the things you said
and all the things you didn't
have the courage to do.
One day you'll realize what you've done,
but by then it will be too late,
and I'll be far gone.
I hope you read this book and know
how much you've hurt me.

But our past will not determine my future,
because I don't intend to repeat history.
I'm stopping the cycle you've continued.
Maybe one day you'll see clearly
how you've let me down,
how you've broken me.
But I can't hold onto hope,
because it's become a heavy weight
that I don't have the strength to carry.
I'll spend the rest of my life
repairing the damage you've done,
and you'll never have the guts to see
that you were the one who ruined me.
I'll take plaster to my walls
and mend the curtains of my girlhood,
hoping desperately
to get back what you've taken from me.
And I'd wish you the best,
but the best was with me,
and that's something you could never see.

SHADOWS IN THE WINDOW

10/31/18
10:41 am

It's Halloween
but you are the only thing that scares me
amongst men and children
dressed as ghosts and skeletons.

You are the monster under my bed,
the nightmare that disrupts my sleep,
the villain in my carefully crafted fantasies.

I know you,
but you are somehow so unfamiliar.
So distant,
a figure that's become unrecognizable to me.

You convinced me
that I was worth nothing.
Perhaps because that's the way you see me:
worth nothing,
holding no value to your legacy.

TREASURE HUNTER

10/30/18
11:25 pm

You drank alcohol
as if the bottle held
some sort of treasure
at the bottom.

You were always so desperate
to see what it held inside.
But I guess one
was never enough to satisfy.

I hope you find
what you've been looking for.
But I think you were only ever
looking for the liquid inside,
never anything more.

I guess that gave you
some sort of contentment
your family couldn't restore.

WAS IT TRUE?

11/2/18
3:52 pm

"I love you."

Those three words
never sounded as empty
as when you said them to me.

Those words,
so easy to say,
but so hard for you to demonstrate.

DISPLACED EMPATHY

You cried so easily
at movies,
but you wouldn't shed a tear
as I poured my heart out to you
in complete and utter defeat.

11 INWOOD OAKS

Are you sure you want to publish
these poems about your dad?

I responded to my mother assuredly:
If he didn't want me to write so poorly about him,
then he shouldn't have done what he did.

That's the thing about writers;
we aren't so quick to forget.
We have a gift of transforming memories
into artistry, a literary tapestry,
mere words laced together
to form intricate stories
to share with the world.
So I write about everything,
the good and bad,
because by using my voice proudly,
someone else will gain the courage to speak.

I will no longer be silenced
simply because people don't like me
speaking on things they deem
should be kept inside, unwritten.
It's my story,
I lived it;
no one else can tell me what to do with it.

People often told me
I was overreacting,
I didn't have it that bad.
They told me to be thankful —
at least I have a dad.
But why should I be thankful
when all he does is laugh
any time I speak?
Finding fault in every sentence,
he'd mock and ridicule me.
Is that how a father ought to be?
Physically present but emotionally absent,
paying no mind to his child's needs,
only caring for himself and tending
to his addiction?

He constantly critiqued me,
my every move,
every word I would speak.
He challenged me on everything I would say
and always had a way
of turning a conversation back to him
and his "good old days."
He never bothered to ask me questions
about my life or my day.
We only exchanged a few sentences
to each other every day.

And somehow he always found a way
to blame me
for his inability
to be a father to me;
for his inability
to be a parent
and care about his child
the way he should.
He told me I was just going through a phase,
and one day I'd come around.
He made me feel like it was my responsibility
to build a relationship with him.
And by the time I was old enough to see
the frailty of our unity,
it was too late to build a relationship
we were in desperate need of *rebuilding*.

And you made it my duty
to rebuild a relationship I never broke,
to repair the heart that you didn't nurture.
We planted a garden of flowers together,
and you let them all die.
Now all that remains are dirt and weeds.

He told me that I had to put forth the effort,
even though he put forth none.
A child isn't meant
to build a relationship
with their parent.

He had it all backwards.
And he lost his chance
to know his one and only daughter,
all because he was too lazy to pursue me.
He made me beg and plead for a relationship,
all the while making empty promises
that he'd never keep.
He swore to me he'd try
after asking over and over again
for the reason why.
And that's all I asked of him, to try,
to see effort on his behalf —
but that was too much to ask.

I will no longer take the blame
for all that he didn't do.
And I won't feel sorry
for speaking my truth.
He hurt me,
knowingly,
relentlessly.
His calloused hands
scarred me.
He tried to convince me
that he didn't hurt me,
and I told him
he didn't get to say that.
He wasn't allowed to claim that.
He couldn't tell me that wasn't true.
You can't just tell someone
"I never hurt you"
when they're wailing and telling you how you did.

Even after all the arguing was through,
it never seemed to stick.
He was so quick to forget his wrongdoings,
but always kept score and made note
of my mistakes.
He'd use them as bait
to start a fight
or to bring up when I'd already been pummeled
beneath the weight of his words.
He was an expert at manipulation,
but so incompetent when it came to apologizing.

He never seemed to understand
just how much he hurt me.
Maybe after reading this book
he'll finally see.
So don't blame me,
because I tried.
I tried so many times,
I begged
and I cried.

I attempted to explain
how he could make it right,
but he never tried.
He was too caught up in his own world,
trying to live like a teenager
at the age of 65.
So I don't regret for one second
all the words that have overflowed
from my chest —
they're all true.

Straight from the heart
that's been broken by you,
here are my words
meant precisely for you.

The cries from the mouth
of a battered little girl
are now the refined poems
of a tattered woman.

And I'll be known as just
another girl with daddy issues.

I've become a *statistic*
    in a diagnostic manual,
        all because of you.

BARTENDER

He only cared about
Hennessy,
Chardonnay,
and Brandy.
All other women were unimportant to him, including me.

EGOCENTRIC

I tried to tiptoe around
you,

Just to please
you,

But nothing was ever enough for
you,

And I suppose I wasn't either.

DOES YOUR MOM KNOW
THE KIND OF MAN YOU ARE?

Thank you for teaching me
exactly who I don't want to be.

Thank you for showing me
that I am strong enough to leave people like you.

This book was never meant
to revolve around you,
but here it is,
going in circles
unintentionally.

You take up so much space in my head,
I should start charging you utilities.
But you're living here rent-free,
taking more than you could ever give to me.

Evidence of your impact on me,
I'll file away for when I need to prove my case.

And after all you've put me through,
I should hate you.
But no matter how hard I try to,
a part of me will always love you.

The younger version of me
that can't bear to lose you
is still clinging to the hope that you'll learn
to be better than you've been,
that somehow you'll change
and shed your skin.

I'll always care for you,
and I'll always love a part of you,
the part of you in our history that seemed decent,
the part that I wish was more than a fraction.

But mostly I cling to my love
for the theoretical version of you,
the idea of who you could have been,
but never were.

So I'll watch movies
and television shows
and I'll cry
at commercials
and wonder
what it's like to love so deeply.

And I'd thank you for making me stronger,
but I was a child —
I didn't need to be strong,
I needed to be loved.

I deserved to be loved
and nurtured
and adored.

I deserved so much more
than what you gave me.

But your pockets were empty
when it came to me,
no love,
no empathy.
You were spent on childish things.

I was forced to learn how to live,
how to be,
without you,
while you stood right in front of me,
watching for when I'd fail
so you could ridicule me.

I had to be my own hero,
my own savior,
when *you should've been mine.*
I had to be stronger
to survive.

I had to learn how to endure
being under your thumb,
a perpetual disappointment.
I had to rebuild
what you broke in me.

With no help from you,
I took the damage
and painted over it
in a shade of dark blue.

I'll say thank you for one thing
and one thing only.

Thank you
for making me who I am today,
a strong woman who no longer tolerates
the unkindness you put me through,
especially from men like you.

Now I have two final questions for you:

Does your mother know the kind of man you are?
And if she does,
how has she stomached you thus far?

SCISSORS

It's okay
to cut off
toxic people.
Lovers,
friends,
family,
whoever it might be.
No matter who tells you otherwise,
it's your life
and your right
to say who is allowed in it.
Someone who has hurt you
and remains unapologetic
shouldn't have access to you.
Boundaries are hard to make,
but they're vital for your protection.
And people who are incapable of change
are not worth the time it takes
to try and explain why they ought to.
They simply don't see the problem
in the things they do.
So allow people in who care about you.
Let in people who are good and kind,
people who show you that you're easy to love.
It's not easy making and upholding boundaries,
but it's *necessary*.
It may hurt the person when you cut them off,
but if it protects you, that's all that matters.

Avoiding the continual damage
being done to you is worth the cost
of pissing the perpetrator off.
Let them learn —
let them be *taught* —
that actions have consequences.
So what if they get their feelings hurt?
You'll gain more than you lost
when you lose someone
without whom you're better off.
And still, people will say it's okay
to cut off bad people,
so long as it's not family,
because family is blood,
and that means everything.
They'll say I'm being harsh and unkind.
You mean…
kind of like the way they've treated me?
Or am I simply enforcing a consequence
that you dislike because it isn't enabling
their mistreatment of me?
The blood of the covenant
is thicker than the water of the womb,
so the saying goes.
So no one can tell me that
chosen bonds aren't more valuable
than my pedigree.

Yet they'll continue to tell me that
I can't simply cut off
toxic family members.
To them I say,
watch me.

UNWORTHY

12/8/18
10:37 pm

You don't deserve
all the words
I've written about you,
but I can't help but write the truth.

Maybe I write so much about you
in hopes that I'll find peace,
but somehow I never do.

No amount of words
will ever be able to rid me of you.

MY DREAMS CAN COME TRUE, AND THEY WILL, IN SPITE OF YOU

1/20/19
1:07 pm

It may be difficult
but it won't be impossible,
even though you convinced me it was.
you made me question all that I believe in,
but I can't carry the weight of doubt
you placed on my shoulders.

I try to recite affirmations in the mirror,
but they all feel like lies.
And I want to find the way back to myself,
but it's a long road to drive.
So I travel with my hazards on,
afraid of what's to come,
because I know there's no version of me
that's untainted by you,
and still, I yield to hope
that somehow you'll come through
and be a better man
for me
and *for you.*

But you never do.

Overanalyze

When I feel I've found my way back
to a version of me that's less damaged by you,
I'm surprised to find it's all smoke and mirrors,
distracting me from your cruelty.

You've left a permanent mark on me,
and I'll never see a version of me
unscathed by the only version of you
I ever knew.

I hope to one day
love myself again,
like I did when I was a little kid
playing dress-up and strumming my purple guitar.
But those days feel so far away,
as if they were from another life,
and in some ways, I suppose they are.

I want to feel confident in my skin
like I did before I was 10,
when I wouldn't look in the mirror
to pick out my flaws,
back when I didn't have the time
to count them all.

And right when I start to feel whole again,
those words come creeping in,
the insecurity you've instilled in me,
and there's no way to rid myself
of your ridicule.

My brain is unable to shake the memory of you.
And I try to convince myself they aren't true,
all the lies you sold me as truth,
but they feel true,
because once upon a time they were
the only certainty I knew.

You convinced me that I'd be a failure,
that my dreams were foolish to pursue,
but I suppose yours were too.
And you made me out to be like you,
but I'm nothing like you,
and that's my favorite thing about me.

I'll never be like you.
I once craved your approval,
your affection,
your tender adoration
that never came to fruition.

I've had big dreams in my life,
but one of my biggest
was to be loved by you,
and that's a dream that can never come true.
So I'll spend my time
pursuing fruitful dreams
that I'll achieve
without any help from you.

I don't need your approval;
I'll be good enough for me,
despite never being good enough for you.

And I'll achieve all my dreams laid before me.
I am capable of doing everything you told me
I couldn't.
I am who I am today,
living in contrast to who
you told me I ought to be.

I'll be me,
because I never wish to be you,
and my dreams can come true,
and *they will, in spite of you.*

ASHTRAYS IN MY HEART

His words
were empty,
just like his heart.

He could never
keep his promises
and ended up
tearing me apart.

Now I just have ashes in my chest
where love was supposed to exist —
your love for me...
Instead it's only remnants,
only secondhand smoke
from your negligence.

DESIGNATED DESTINY

1/20/19
3:29 pm

If I could change anything,
I would change my relation to you.
That is the curse I have been given.
I can change my last name,
but that wouldn't change my genetics.
And I know,
despite my DNA,
I don't have to be like you,
for I am your legacy,
but *you are not mine.*
You are just a rotting branch in my family tree,
with shriveled leaves,
slowly decaying away,
leaving sickness in your wake.

I'll find real love one day,
and all the tears I've cried over you
will become a distant memory.

And the only thing
we'll ever have in common
is one surname
that can *easily be changed.*

ORPHAN

I might not have a father's love,
but I have The Father's love,
and that'll *have to be enough.*

LOOK AT ME NOW

I told him I wanted to publish a book.
He looked at me with a harshness in his eyes
and said *it'll never happen.*
Those words rang in my head.
But he doesn't know what I'm capable of,
not now and certainly not then.
He crushed my dreams once again,
smiting any remaining hope I had.
But I will be a published author.
In spite of him.
In spite of his words.
In spite of his doubts.
So look at me now.
Look at all that I've done
despite your doubts.
I made it here somehow.
You gave me the seeds of doubt
and watered them daily,
but I've uprooted the plant
and thrown it out.
You don't get a say now.
My dreams were always worthy,
despite what you said about them.
And I am good enough,
even though you never thought I could be.

VERACITY

I could write him
the way I wish he was,
but that would be a lie to conserve.

So I choose to write him
the way he is,
because that's what he deserves.

BETTER OFF

You were supposed to be there for me,
but when I needed you the most
you just walked out on me.

Leaving was the only thing you were good at.

You were never there,
not really.
Now all I have is the memory of you
to sit with and grieve.

I don't know what it's like to be you,
and honestly, I don't wish to.
I don't think I want to understand you,
because understanding the depths of your cruelty —
the *reasoning* and *justifying* —
would make me just as culpable as you.

I tried to please you.
I tried to make you proud of me.
But satisfying you
was something I could never achieve.

You said you loved me,
but how can you love someone
you don't even know?
And what you did to me wasn't love,
not in my dictionary,
not in any dictionary.

The pictures of you are now filed away,
a face that serves as a reminder of all that I lost
and all that I never had.

You weren't a father to me,
you were merely an absentee
in my life and upbringing.

I needed more than a fantasy of who you could be.
I didn't need an idealized version of you
in my dreams,
I needed the real thing.
And to think that
I once thought it was a possibility,
having you the way I dreamed…
Only made me feel naive.

I know the contents of a bottle
are more filling than I could ever be,
but maybe if you got to know me
you'd see things differently.

People tell me it's fun to party,
to drink,
to smoke,
to experiment.
But I can't see it that way,
not after seeing what it did to our family.

All I see are people desperate for an escape,
so they'll do anything
to distract themselves from reality.
And I get it,
believe me.
But I couldn't end up like you;
I refuse to.

And I don't think I'll ever fully understand
all that you did.

I was just a kid...
why did you expect so much from me?

Now I'm left feeling so incomplete,
simply because you placed
the weight of the world on me.

I'm better off without you,
who will forever remain
a stain on my family tree.

FALSE HOPE

Thanks for the flowers, I guess.
But they won't make up for your mess.

BRIDGES YOU'VE BURNED

2/17/19
3:08 pm

You are so self-centered.
What do you see
when you stare at yourself
in the mirror?

Because when I look at you,
all I see is someone
who never cared about me.

You're so in love
with your reflection,
a modern Narcissus,
with no moral compass.

I don't know what you find
worth reflecting upon.
To me, all I see is an unfamiliar face
who doesn't know what love means.

The bridge to Hope
has already been burned,
and you were the one
who lit the match.

But you blamed me
for the fire you started.

PSYCHOLOGY

2/17/19
3:17 pm

I have daddy issues.
What else is new?

So much for all those therapy
Sessions I went to.

It was never enough
To make me forget you.

Nothing will ever rid me
Of the scars you've left.

They are stuck on me
Like a tattoo.

EMPTY APOLOGIES

You mock and ridicule me
As I'm sat in the back
While you're driving.

Tears are slowly streaming
Down my face
As you make yourself the victim.

You blame her
And make her apologize
For asking you to say sorry to me.

You could never apologize to me
Because you never
Found fault in your actions.

Your apologies are overused and insincere.
I'm tired of spending all these years
Wasting all these tears on you.

ORANGE

2/21/19
8:23 pm

I now know why I hate that color —
It reminds me of you.
That color has been *burned* into my memory.
And just like the baggage I carry,
It's all because of you.

I FORGAVE YOU

Right there,
in that moment,
I forgave you.

As he looked at me
while I was crying,
he asked, *What did I ever do*
to hurt you?
I broke down and refused.
That was the last time
I ever tried to talk to you.

You told me you didn't hurt me
while I cried at your feet,
yelling about all the pain
you'd inflicted upon me.
But still, you refuted every claim,
telling me my memories
were mere delusions.

Right there,
in that moment,
I refused.

I refused to ever let another tear
fall from my eyes due to you.

You died that day.
At least *you died to me.*
So I bury the hurt,
the pain,
and our memories,
along with you.
And that's the only place
you will ever stay with me.

Within these pages,
I have showcased my hurt.
But you still
can't see it, can you?
Do you think you're guiltless?
How dare you.

Look what you put me through.
I went through hell because of you.
But you still can't see the truth.
You're blinded by the lies
you convinced yourself were true.
You convinced me
it was my fault
that you didn't want me.

And now you can't make it up to me.
It's too late for you to do anything,
not that you would, anyway.
And now I don't even want you to.
I wanted a father who cared,
but you were never there.

If you're reading this, Dad,
I'm sorry.
I'm sorry that I wasn't enough.
I'm sorry that you never cared.
I'm sorry you were never there.
I'm sorry,
but you're too late.
I'm sorry,
because one of us has to be,
so I guess it'll have to be me.

CATASTROPHIC HEARTBREAK

Sometimes silence
Can be the most catastrophic
Form of heartbreak.

The words lessen more
With each passing day,

Yet you still blamed me
For all the words
You could never say.

DO YOU EVER THINK OF ME?

2/25/20
8:27 pm

How twisted can you be?
To think you needed an invitation
to have a relationship with me,
your daughter?
Your only excuse was that you thought
I was going through a passing phase.
How does that make it okay?

Yes, it's true,
I didn't like you
because you didn't give a damn about me.
You never asked me about my life,
yet somehow it's my fault
that I didn't ask you about yours.

I was a child,
but you gave me
the responsibility of an adult.
You were supposed to love me
unconditionally, but you left me.

And you can't do anything now
to make up for all the wasted years
and my thousands of tears.
It's too late.

But I guess you were never trying in the first place.
You placed all the responsibility
for our failed relationship on me.
But this is all on you.

You were the adult.
It was your responsibility
to love and pursue me,
but you did neither.

You told me,
inaudibly,
that you never cared about me
because action speaks louder than words.
And in this case,
there were neither.

No actions,
no words,
only tears,
one shattered heart,
and a broken little girl
who is now a jaded woman.

So I have one final question for you:
Do you ever think of me,
and regret anything?

RIVERS BETWEEN US

6/13/18
10:24 pm

I still think about you
and what could have been.
I still wonder why you left
and never wanted to see me again.

Many people have left me,
but I wasn't expecting
one of them to be you…
I'm well acquainted
with people leaving,
but it doesn't make it hurt
any less when they do.

What did I do wrong?
Was it something I said?
Your name will forever
echo in my head.

We talked about going to university
together and getting an apartment.
I guess plans change
and people do too.
I've had my heart broken by only one man,
but it's been shattered by many friends.
Why did you have to be one of them?

Without any explanation
you left me empty-handed
with nothing to show
for the years
we spent together.
You abandoned me
like an old T-shirt
you no longer wanted.
I was too worn and faded.
Did you leave because I was already so jaded?

Why did this happen?
Why didn't you want me anymore?
After two years, what made you
give up on me?
You left silently.
No rationale,
no reasoning,
nothing to justify
your sudden absence,
but *there it was,*
    lingering
        in the air between us.

I heard whispers
from our mutual friends
about what you thought of me,
your true feelings.

I wish you had just talked to me —
I'd have resolved any problems willingly.
I would've done just about anything
to keep you in my life.
Now I'm fighting with a ghost,
begging to know
the reason you let go.

LAUREN

6/14/18
10:32 am

Do you remember the day we saw each other
in the grocery store after months apart?

Because I do.

I will never forget that moment.
I was with my mom,
you were with your dad.
We saw each other across the store
and ran to embrace each other
like we had been apart for years
instead of just weeks and months.

We cried in the middle of the store.
I'm sure people thought we were crazy,
but I didn't care
because I was with you.
I was in your arms again,
in the arms of my best friend,
the closest thing I've had to a sister.

Tears rolled down my cheeks out of happiness.
I was so happy to see you,
to hear your voice.

God, I missed you.

It's been five years since then,
and still I miss you.
I'm sorry things ended the way they did.
I wish I knew why.

Was I too overbearing?
Did I annoy you?
Did I worry too much?
I know that's a problem I have.
I can't help it.
I wish you didn't leave.

I asked Maggie how you were,
because even though
you might not have cared back then,
I did.
I still do.
I think a part of me always will,
and I hope you do too.

The thought haunts me at night,
wondering what I did to make you leave.
But I understand;
I can be a bit too much sometimes,
even for me, so it's no surprise, really.
But still, I wish you had given me a reason,
an explanation, anything.

A part of me was angry with you
for so many years
because I didn't understand why
you abandoned our friendship.

I was mad, but more than that,
I was heartbroken.
You knew how much heartbreak
I had faced in my life,
how hard it was for me to trust people,
all the friends who had left me.
I never thought you'd join the list.
I hope you remember the good days,
the good times we had together.
Please remember me for those times.

And if by some twist of fate
we meet again someday...
know that I'll always save a place
for you right next to me.

SUMMERTIME AND SLEEPOVERS WITH YOU

Wherever you are,
whoever you're with,
I hope that you're happy.
I hope you're content.
Please remember me
from the days when we
laughed and smiled.
I hope you still think about me too
because not a day goes by
that I forget you.
I want you to be happy,
and I'm sorry it couldn't be
with me.
I still think about you
and wonder how you're doing.
You were the only one
who left me without reason
that I would want back.
I'd welcome you with open arms,
a forgiving heart, listening ears
because a part of my heart
will always belong to you.
In the palm of your hands it resides.
So please take care of me
the way I wanted to take care of you.

RIVERS BETWEEN US II

I recall the day
we saw each other
for the first time in months.
I will forever treasure
that moment I saw you
from a distance
and we ran to each other
and I jumped into your arms.
It was that cliché moment
of seeing a friend
you haven't seen
in years,
but for us,
it had only been weeks.
It was a genuine feeling
of missing you
and being so excited
to reunite.
We started to cry together,
tears of pure joy,
a female experience
I'll never forget,
one of girlhood
and happiness.
We hadn't seen each other
since school ended for summer.
I was so ecstatic to see you,
and you were overjoyed
to see me.

That's one of my favorite memories
with you,
along with the one where
you crawled into bed
with me
the morning after our sleepover.
You had slept in my brother's old room
and when you awoke
you came to wake me.
You got under the sheets
and we watched a new music video
on your phone, from the boy band
everyone raved about.
And I remember feeling so content,
unlike any happiness I'd felt before.
This was so much more…
I kept the headband you left at my house;
I didn't have the heart to
give it back to you.
I still have it, even now.
The only remnant of you
that I can cling to…
from when we were happy,
when my future included you.
I still love you.
I always will.
You were my best friend
my sister
my confidant
my closest ally.
I'd have done anything to keep
you by my side.

But I understand now,
people grow apart
sometimes.
But I would've stayed with you
for a lifetime.
Would you have done the same?
If given the opportunity,
would you go back
and change our fate?
I know it's useless
to live in the past,
but I spend most of my free time there.
And I can't help but wonder
if you think of me…
If you do, I just hope
you think of me fondly.

HENRIK

6/13/18
10:11 pm

You told me I had a beautiful soul.
I didn't believe you at first.
I thought you were only joking
so I laughed.
You got mad at me for doing that.
Only then did I realize
you were serious.
You meant it.
I apologized and laughed
nervously, confused
by your unique compliment
but felt moved at the same time.

I looked up at his face concerned,
not for him, but myself.
I didn't know what to do with what he said,
so I did nothing.
I had received compliments before,
but none close to this caliber.

I was taken aback by the feeling
of being admired by someone
for something other than my appearance.

It's a compliment that's stuck with me
ever since.
Never in my life
has someone looked at me
and admired *my heart,*
my brain,
my soul,
and audibly stated so.
To think that the most *innate* part of me,
the *deepest,*
the most *private* and *sacred* part
was *beautiful,*
was a profound thing to me.
And I didn't know how to respond.
There's no response
that could paint the feeling
in my heart
or the thoughts running rampant
in my head.
I was in awe of your affection,
and I wish I knew what you meant by it,
what prompted you to say it…
but I was too afraid to ask.
I looked into his blue eyes
and he grinned at me, then walked away
as if it was the most normal thing to say
as if he hadn't just
completely wrecked my world
with a mere sentence.
He left me standing in the hallway,
perplexed and wildly empowered.

I don't think he knows
the weight of his words
and how they changed my world.
I will always remember
the way he made me feel that day.
It felt like a dream.
I felt lost in a daze.
The words that escaped your lips
were so tender,
so sweet, for a boy
who was only in his teens.
Dripping with a French accent,
you were a foreign exchange student
and I reasoned that perhaps
it's commonplace in France
to speak in such a way.
You'll probably never know
just how much those words meant
or how much time I've spent
thinking of them.
It's been half a decade since then
since you uttered those words to me
outside my English class
and left me in a tizzy.
Five years since you said
those five words:
"You have a beautiful soul."
And of all the kind remarks I've received,
yours hasn't been beat.

I await the day
someone sweeps me off my feet
and gives me a compliment just as sweet.
But for now, yours will remain my favorite,
the best I've ever received.
Thank you for saying that to me
with the utmost sincerity.
Thank you, you beautiful
ginger-haired boy
with a heart of gold
and a soul to match.
You helped change the way I see myself
in the best way possible.
My soul will always be beautiful,
not because you said it was,
simply *because it is,*
so thank you for being
one of the first people to notice.

WHY DID I LET YOU HURT ME?

some words don't deserve to see the light of day,
and mine for you will remain that way.

ME, MYSELF, AND MY INADEQUACY

6/1/18
10:47 pm

Your skin is flawless and beautifully tinted,
while mine is pale and lifeless.
Not a single blemish can be seen on your forehead,
while mine is a minefield of scars and imperfections.
Your dimples fit your cheeks oh, so perfectly,
while mine only exists on one side,
completing me unevenly.
Stubble sits on your face with a sparse patch on the side,
which always made you a little insecure,
but I love the way it feels upon my cheek.

You are everything to me —
at least I think you could be.

Imperfections adorn every part of my being,
while you look like a work of art that belongs in a museum.
The years have not been kind to me; they've scarred me,
but they appear to have been kind to you.
And I'm jealous of the way the sun kisses your face,
leaving you tanned a darker shade,
while I only get sunburnt a tone of red.
People have always left me when given the chance —

I wonder if you'd do the same...
would you leave me behind,
adding a new scar to my collection?
I *could* love you, but I don't think you could love me.
And no matter how hard I try,
I'll never be enough for you,
but you will always be
more than enough for me.

DAYLIGHT DREAMING

I had a dream last night.
It wasn't a dream I wish to remember,
it was a nightmare I want to forget.
You were there,
but not how I hoped you'd be.
You weren't mine
the way you ought to be.
And seeing you happy, without me,
broke me.
My heart shattered
when I saw the way
you held her in your arms.
You looked at her the way
I wished you'd look at me.
Hurt and betrayed,
I turned away.
You were never mine... but I wanted you to be.
In my wildest fantasies,
you were meant to end up with me.
I want you to be happy,
but I wish it was with me.
And I don't understand
why it hurts so much to see
you with someone else
when you never belonged to me.
How can I lose something I never had?
Somehow, I did, when I lost you.

I wanted you,
every *ounce*,
every *bit*.
I wanted you
even when you were tired,
angry,
sick.
But even in my dreams,
I can't have you,
because *you were never mine to lose.*

M.O.M.

It's hard to conceive
that three letters could create
something, someone,
so wonderful and full of beauty.
I have known the *truest*
and *purest* love thanks to you.
When you held me as a baby
and looked down at me,
admiring my beauty,
I can assure you I was looking up at you
and thinking the same thing:
You were the most beautiful thing I would ever see.
From day one you treasured me,
as if you held in your arms
the most precious thing
this world had ever seen.
And looking up at you I saw my whole world
right there, in front of my very eyes.

You taught me to laugh, to love,
but you weren't the one who taught me
what it meant to leave,
and I'll be forever grateful
that you stayed…
when it was hard, when it was easy,
when it was hell, you remained.

You taught me so many things,
but I'm most grateful for the knowledge
you introduced to me
of God and his divine work in me,
because I can see it in you too.
The beauty of divinity
exists in the green of your eyes,
the scars on our bodies,
reminders of what we've survived.
And we have matching marks on our hearts
from the same man
who was incapable of loving us
the way we deserved.
And I know you're too selfless to be selfish
so you'd do it all over again to have me,
but if the choice were mine,
I'd go back in time
and rid you of the future
you're living.

I'd set up a better timeline
where I'd never be yours
but you'd always be mine.
I'd sacrifice my life for your happiness
time and time again
I wouldn't hesitate to change the storyline
so you never met him
and I'd save you from the catastrophe,
at the cost of me,
but I wouldn't mind.

Still, despite these wishes
I know there's no guarantee
my efforts would change anything,
because even if things were different
there's nothing absolute,
and there's still the possibility that
with a different plot,
the ending may be an unchangeable fate.
So when we grieve together
over all that we lost and all we never had,
I remind you,
just because things could've been different
doesn't mean they'd be better.
And there's no point in reliving
the events that have transpired
because I can't change them,
no matter how much I wish to
for you…
And still, we do,
we reminisce on all the hellfire
we've walked through, me and you.

You've shown me what it means
to love selflessly, sacrificially,
so you can't blame me
for learning from your teachings.
You showed me the kindness of your heart,
and I'd like to think there's the same kindness in mine,
the same willingness and enthusiasm
to help and comfort others,
to stand up for others and myself.

You showed me how to show kindness
to those who don't deserve it,
and I taught you that you don't always have to.
You've shown me how to laugh in the face of adversity
and have joy amidst chaos.
And I've seen your anxiety
that's now present in me,
that you try to hide so carefully,
so you bottle it away for no one else to see,
but it's evident to me.
You've taught me to enjoy every little moment
and cherish the time spent with friends and family.

With you, every moment is special,
every grocery store trip
is an adventure,
every chore, a chance to bond
and laugh.
Because you're my mother,
I know the statement printed on mugs is true
when it comes to you:
You are the best mom in the entire world.
My admiration for you is boundless,
my love for you is endless,
my heart is forever tethered to you,
and I wouldn't want it any other way.
You are *my person…*
the one I run to when I'm in need,
when I'm down further than I thought I could be,
when I need a hug,
when I need to cry,
you're always there for me.

I could write endlessly of my love for you,
filling up pages and books of my adoration,
but I'll summarize my emotions with one last thing:
You are my sunshine
   you make me happy
      when skies are gray
         may you always know, dear,
           how much I love you...

TEARS IN THE BATHROOM

You've changed,
but then again, so have I.
And that's not necessarily a bad thing.
Change is growing
towards who you're meant to be.
And sometimes people aren't meant to be
on that journey with you.
You can outgrow people sometimes,
I've found this to be true.
I can't recognize the person I see
when I look at you.

You've changed
    your hair,
        your clothes,
            your mindset.

You act as if you are on top
of the world, although inside
you're miserable.
And I hated to see you go,
but I had to stop holding on
to something that was no longer there.

I clung onto you,
onto us,
with my life.

I pleaded with you,
begging to get you back.

We talked for hours,
which only resolved minutes.
You chose someone else,
and this I had to live with.

Although I no longer have you,
I still have many people
who love me.
But it won't be the same.
It'll never be the way you loved me.

I know I didn't need our friendship
to complete me, but a part of me
feels missing,
because without you,
I don't know what to do.
I gave so much of myself to you,
and now it's gone forever.
All the time I spent with you,
the times I confided in you,
are all memories now,
lost in the ether of our youth.

Loving you helped me find happiness
I didn't know could exist.
Losing you helped me come to terms
with the potential temporality of it.

In loving you and losing you I learned
the importance of boundaries
and the vitalness of letting go,
but I'm one hell of a grudge-holder,
so I'm still grappling with the undertow.

And yes, I still think of you.
I still wonder what could have been...
but now all that we've had remains
in the past, a disappearing
image in the distance,
slowly fading out of focus.

I HOPE SHE MAKES YOU HAPPY

Apologies full of meaningless
phrases said one too many times.
I can no longer see the hurt
in your eyes, but I can
assure the anger and pain
are visible in mine.
I gave you so many chances,
but they never made a difference.
I poured out my heart to you,
crying, hoping
this time you'd come through.
It was time
for me to say goodbye.

Trying to force something to keep living
that was meant to die was killing me.
It was a hopeless dispute,
no more time and effort could I afford
to expend.
I stopped sitting at home alone on Saturday nights
looking at your pictures on Instagram,
wondering why I wasn't invited.
You abandoned me
for something shiny and new,
people who were easier, livelier than me.
And I don't understand how
you could be so heartless,
and I don't think I'd ever want to.
I would never do the things you did.

I would never leave someone
who told me how afraid they were
of opening up, how terrified
they were of people leaving.
    But that's what you did to me.
And I hate to think
you were one of the best things
in my life, once upon a time...

J & B

To my uncles:

Thank you for being good.
Thank you for being
who I needed you to be.
Thank you for showing me
that not all men
are apathetic
and untrustworthy.
Thank you for being
the kind of men
I wanted my father to be.
I don't think you'll ever know
just how much,
but I appreciate you
for being men
I can look up to.

MY HEART, HIS HANDS, MY FANTASIES

1/8/19
12:21 pm

I had a dream that you were with me.
I was curled up in your arms,
sleeping peacefully.
You brushed my hair
from my face and placed it
delicately behind my ear.
Your eyes met mine
and sparkled in the sunlight.
My hand rested
on your bare chest
as yours held me
tightly against you.
I looked up at your beautiful
golden skin
and you smiled at me so brightly,
for a moment the sunlight dimmed.
A soft smile, just wide enough
for your dimples to show on each cheek.
Simply imagining your presence
made me feel complete.
I know I could love you
for the rest of my days.
With your hands on my waist,
gripping me so tight
I know this would be worth the fight.
Maybe one day
I'll gain the courage to say hi.

ROMEO ~~AND JULIET~~

12/13/18
10:46 pm

You told me you loved me,
I said I love you too
just not in the way
that you wanted me to.

FOR THE GIRL I LOVED IN HIGH SCHOOL

As my hands intertwined with hers
in the dimly lit auditorium, I felt happiness
unlike any I'd felt before,
a resounding sense of peace
knowing I had her.
Inside her blue eyes,
a light shone as she looked at me.
I loved her with my whole heart.
Not the romantic kind of love
that makes your palms sweaty;
it was the kind of love that makes you feel
warmth in your belly.
The love of a friend,
the comfort of their embrace,
the feeling of closeness
nothing else could replicate —
a love that feels like a soulmate.
The platonic love
that feels special,
once-in-a-lifetime,
is the kind of love I felt
for her.
I never knew soulmates
could be found in friendships too.
And what a beautiful revelation it was,
knowing you were one of mine,
once upon a time.

She was all that I wanted
all that I needed,
everything I'd hoped for,
everything I ever imagined
a friend to be.
I felt safe
next to her, I was comforted
by her laughter,
content at the sight of her smile.
I loved her,
and I always will.
But our story didn't end well,
not like in movies or fairytales.
We didn't have a happy ending.
And although it wasn't
a Shakespearean tragedy,
it felt that way at 17.
We went our separate ways,
and I suppose it was for the best,
but I still wish to this day
things stayed the same.
I wish we didn't drift apart
and give in to the inevitability
of unavailability
that occurs when you grow older.
I wish there wasn't a divide between us,
separating us from what we were,
and more than anything,
I wish I hadn't pushed you away.
I should've begged you to stay.

But I was hurt,
and I was stubborn,
and losing you will forever be
one of my greatest mistakes.
I let misunderstandings
get in the way,
and my pride was too high
to call it even and start anew.
But what hurt the most
was how she claimed you
for keeps, after
treating you and me equally.
The pain was all the same
at the end of the day.
And from where I stood,
it looked like you chose her too.
After all that we'd been through,
you chose the girl who hurt both me and you,
and I can't seem to get that through
the pain in my chest
from my youth.
And I know I'm too young to be so bitter,
but I can't help it.
I'm too far gone to quit
holding grudges, I've obtained
too many to stop now.
It's become a collection.
And Madeline,
I know I was out of line.

I was angry for a while,
confused,
but enough time
has passed that I can see
through the haze
of my early days
and see clearly the simplicity
of camaraderie.
And I miss how simple it was,
you and me,
and even her too,
before things got so messed up,
before you stayed
and I left.
I couldn't take the pressure caving in on me.
And I became a version of me
I'm now ashamed of.
I wish we had made up.
I wish I didn't leave.
I wish I was mature enough
to see the forest for the trees.
And I wish I didn't miss you
as much as I do,
still hung up on adolescence,
denying the inevitable truth.
And I didn't expect it to hurt as much as it did
when you moved southeast of Lake Michigan.
But it hurt like hell
and my bones ache when
I think of you.

When I miss you,
I think of that Halloween
at a mutual friend's house
watching a horror movie,
sitting so close, gripping tightly
to each other's hand.
I can recall the proximity
and how we joked with each other.
Taking temporary claim,
calling each other "babe"
in the most platonic and playful way.
And you're the only friend who felt that way,
besides our other friend
I spooned with on the couch
after I said I never had,
so she spooned me
while we watched a movie,
and it felt so lovely.
I was never a big fan
of physical gestures or touch, but with you,
with genuine friendship being the root,
it felt comfortable.
I'll always miss the familiarity of you
and your embrace,
the way your face
lit up when you smiled,
the way you made my stomach hurt
from laughing.

I'll miss all the days we spent
being young,
being kids.

You calmed me
with the touch of your hand,
and you loved me
with the kind of love
a sister has,
a love I'd never felt before,
a love I've never felt since...

CUNNING AND BEAUTIFUL

To the girl in high school
who gave herself to boys
who didn't deserve her:
You don't need to search
for the missing pieces
of yourself
in someone else.
You never needed their approval.
You already had everything you needed
right inside of you.
No boy, or drug,
or drink can complete you.
You are whole just as you are,
So stop searching for love
in crowded bars and find it
right where you are.
You are all you need.
I hope one day that'll be enough for you,
and I hope the same for me.

OVERSENSITIVE

2/25/19
8:19 pm

I apologized for what you did.
You somehow convinced me
it was my fault
that you yelled at me so hatefully.
I loved you, and I still do,
but you said I was "too sensitive" for you,
so we haven't spoken since that early summer night.
But, if I'm the sensitive one,
why did a single sentence I uttered
make you explode?
Nonetheless, I'm fine being the
oversensitive one in your narrative.
Besides, I'd rather be tenderhearted than cold.

I care so much about so many things,
and that's precisely the reason
you quit talking to me.
I defend people and I defend myself
because for so much of my life
I had nobody
to fight for me.
So I swing with all my might.
So sue me for thinking
everyone should be treated equally.

What a terrible, awful way to think —
at least, that's what you convinced me.
I no longer care what you think of me.
Because you made it clear a long time ago
that you don't care about me anymore.
I'm sorry I ruined a lifelong friendship,
But it wasn't really my fault…was it?

MICHAEL

I met you freshman year.
You were so sweet,
so caring.
We had art class together.
You sat in the back of the room.
You had lovely tan skin
from playing golf.
Your smile was so soft and perfectly
complemented your kind eyes.
We had a tight-knit group of friends.
And I remember giving out my cherry and lime gum
in math class to Maggie, Katie, Lauren, Kody, and you.
Sometimes I miss those days.
I miss seeing you every day,
knowing you would always be there.
You were one of the only guys in my life
to genuinely care about me.
I miss the days
we would sit together in math class
with our other friends and laugh
at something stupid.
I still remember the day you came to my choir concert.
It meant the world to me.
I'm sorry I didn't say it then,
but I cared so deeply for you.
You were such an incredible friend.
I can't believe we don't talk anymore.
I'm sorry we didn't stay in touch after that first year.

I became a different person,
one I didn't want to become.
Every time I think back to you
I can't help but wonder
what could have been.
Would we still be friends?
You've had a couple girlfriends between now and then,
and they seemed lovely.
I wonder what happened with them.
I guess I'll never know.
Besides, it's not my business to meddle.
But I am cursed with curiosity,
and I want to know about such happenings,
because I believe that you deserve the best things.
You deserve so much happiness and contentment,
and I truly hope you find it.

Sometimes I just miss your company.
The way you would make me laugh,
the way you would actually listen
when I spoke.
But maybe I just miss the history
between you and me.
I miss feeling comfortable around you,
a feeling I don't feel too often
around men.
Thank you for helping write
a beautiful chapter of my life.
You will always hold a special place in my heart.
Thank you for being you, Michael.

MICHAEL II

You were one of the only boys
to never disappoint me.
Thank you for being that person for me,
simply by being you.

CODY WITH A K

I will never be able to forget you,
no matter how hard I try.
I can't believe I used to see you as a friend,
because now I despise you.
I think the reason I was drawn to you at first
was because you reminded me of my dad...
You were mean and cruel.
You made me feel worthless,
and I suppose that was familiar to me,
those feelings,
so I let them wash over me
and confused them with friendship
and chemistry.
You'd call me so many mean things,
but still, there were times you were
there for me when no one else was.
And I remember the night
my mom drove you home,
and you sat in the back seat
while I rode shotgun.
You were so polite,
you played nice,
you even fooled me,
so my mom was always rooting for us two.
But if that ever happened
it would've been me repeating history.
Making the same mistakes as my mother
loving another version of my father.

And now she sees you differently,
and so do I.
The only man she'd want by my side
is a man who would never make me cry.
And you don't fit the requirements.
I heard the whispers about you around school,
the girl you took advantage of,
the real you.
And I was relieved that I had already
distanced myself from you
by the time my intuition proved to be true.
Because before then I kept coming back to you.
I was so young and naive.
I was so dumb to think you could change
and be who I wanted you to be.
And you have changed,
quite drastically,
just not for the better.
We were a powder keg
ready to blow at a moment's notice,
volatile and unhealthy,
but still, I found myself
clinging to the good bits of you,
hoping that was the real side of you.
There were good times between us,
it's true,
but the bad times seemed to
weigh more heavily on me
than they did on you.
And I never thought I'd grow to fear you,
but now I do.
I'm terrified of the person you've become
and I'm mourning the person I thought I knew.

But you showed me who you were
and I believe you.
The red flags were large and plenty,
I just couldn't see past my rose-colored lenses,
but now,
from a distance,
I see it for what it is.
I'm no longer romanticizing your cruelty,
painting it as adoration
when it was nothing more than malice towards me.
Toxic,
unhealthy,
this thing between you and me,
but I colored it differently,
settling for the attention of your unkindness,
assuming it's the only kind I'd ever get.
It was so confusing keeping up with
your ever-changing demeanor
and walking on eggshells to try and keep you happy.

You weren't good for me,
and I was too good for you.
And at the end of the day,
you're just like him,
just like my father —
and that's not a compliment.
You'll always remind me of my dad,
because just like him,
you hurt me,
and left
without a single apology.

GLYNN (ALMOST LOVE)

2/27/19
11:16 am

I never thought I'd find myself
writing these words,
but here I am,
writing them for you.
We have so much history…
I can't help but wonder
if you ever think of me,
because I think of you
often. In so many of my memories,
you're there.
I wonder if I'm in yours too.

I remember it vividly,
the first day I met you.
I was only 5 at the time,
and you walked into my kindergarten classroom
on crutches. You were taller
than everyone else.
Your hair was unkempt
and photobleached.
You were always so nice to me —
even when you would tease me,
there was kindness behind every quip.
I cannot recall a time in my life
that you weren't there too.

Overanalyze

We were so close then,
in elementary school,
when the only pressing decision to make
was who we'd talk to
on the swing set at recess.

I had a crush on your best friend,
then your other friend in middle school.
I wonder how that made you feel.
Looking back, I wonder if you were jealous
of my affections and how they were
never for you.
Now I don't see them the same way I did then.
I looked them up on social media
and I can't believe I ever liked the latter,
while now I find the former's father
more attractive than I do him.
But perhaps that says more about me now,
because back then I loved easily
and freely,
unapologetically.

But my feelings were never requited,
just sat and rotted in my heart
until they fermented into nutrients,
enabling me to love again.
It was never love,
I only convinced myself it was.
I have never loved,
and I fear I never will.
Perhaps that's why I find myself living in the past
and thinking of you more than I ought to.

I hope you're doing well,
better than I am,
better than I've been.
I hope you're happy
and smiling,
contented.
I hope life has been kinder to you
than it has to me.

Your smile always lit up a room.
You left a mark on everyone you met,
a lingering effect,
the way you were,
and I recall it so clearly,
your effervescent charm.

We were so young then.

I remember when I considered us close friends,
when we even called ourselves best friends
on playgrounds and between school bells,
and how you would call me nicknames
that I claimed to hate but never did.
You were the only one I allowed
to call me by that name;
it didn't sound right coming from anyone else.

Now I find myself clinging to unsubstantial things.
I'll assign value to them,
the same way I do memories,
romanticizing things that shouldn't be romanticized.

We were always close,
but I never imagined I'd feel this way about you.
And God, I hope you never read this...
But if you do,
please know I miss you,
because as we grew up, we grew apart.

Even so, you'll always have
a special place in my heart.
You always brought me back
to a time and place
that felt so comfortable,
so safe, it made me nostalgic
for the easier days,
before we had to worry
about bills and salaries.

One day, over a decade ago,
I was with my mom in the grocery store,
and we ran into your mom and little sister.
She talked to my mother about the feelings
you had for me and how you always
talked about me.
We were still kids then,
and I thought nothing of it.
But looking back now, there were so many signs
of your affection for me that I ignored.
What exactly were you waiting for?
Because I didn't know I felt the same way until
the option was off the table...
I was too late.

Seeing you with her hurt me more
than I expected.
I remember looking at your prom pictures,
imagining myself
standing next to you instead.
I knew you liked me,
but it was a thought I let slip in and out
with no effect on me,
because I never saw you that way.

And to be honest,
I didn't think anyone could see me that way,
so I brushed it off like a joke you'd make.

We started talking again in high school.
We had a history class together,
our seats assigned alphabetically,
with you sitting right in front of me.
I was in such a bad place,
and I tried to push you away,
but you remained kind and diligent towards me.
You were so persistent,
it was almost obnoxious
And still, I tried
to make you hate me
so it would be easier on me.
I tried to remedy and reason
why you shouldn't be friends with me,
but you countered my every point,
questioning me,
challenging me.

There was a group of popular girls
sat just in front of us,
your acquaintances.
And any time they'd interact with you,
I was reminded of just how different we were,
the stark divide between you and me,
so evident, so clearly seen.
I tried to convince you
not to talk to me
because you were too popular to be seen
anywhere in my vicinity.

I told you every day
when you would turn around at your desk
to talk to me
that we were in different social brackets,
so we couldn't be friends.
But that didn't stop you from trying.

I didn't want you to sacrifice
your reputation by talking to a girl like me.
I didn't see myself as good enough
to associate with you.
You were well known,
on the football team,
liked by everyone,
and I was a wallflower
going through depression
for the first time at 15.
I couldn't be good for you
when I couldn't even be good for me.

But I don't want you to feel bad —
at the time, I pushed everyone away.
And I could tell you didn't want to
give up on me,
but I made it so hard for you.
I was so hard on you...
And perhaps there was still some
residual anger towards you
about what happened back then,
because I'm nothing if not consistent
when it comes to holding grudges.
But still, you were so kind to me.
And it drove me crazy.

I just wanted you to leave me alone...
because I felt so miserable,
I assumed I ought to be alone;
I didn't want anyone else to share my misery.
I didn't want to burden you
with my suffering.
I tried to convince you
that I hated you,
but I didn't,
and I don't.

That year I was so lost,
confused, and dejected.
I wanted to be alone.
I wanted to disappear.
I wanted to slip away from existence.
And I wanted no witnesses to my demise.
I wanted to be alone as I died.

My first bout of depression hit me hard,
and still, you had a way
of making me forget my misery,
even if only momentarily.
You always managed to make me laugh,
even on my worst days.
You could get me to smile
when all I felt was pain.

Do you remember in math when the teacher got
mad at you for saying "bless you"?
Because I still do!
Someone kept sneezing,
and you kept saying, "Bless you,"
as one might do, the typical reaction,
a reflex to the sound,
and the teacher got annoyed
and told you to leave the room.
I remember the day you complimented me
on my 5 Seconds of Summer T-shirt.
It made me feel like a little kid again,
blushing and feeling acknowledged.
And I never asked anything of you.
I never asked for your saving or your kindness.
You didn't need to rescue me,
so don't feel guilty for being blind to my suffering.
I hid it so well,
even my mother didn't believe me.

Why did you care?
After all the times I was so rude to you...
I pushed you away,
so why did you stay?
Why didn't you
just give up on me?
I know it probably didn't mean anything to you,
but those little things meant more to me
than you'll ever know.

Thank you
for being you.
And I'm sorry
for pushing you away...
because when you finally left,
I realized all I wanted you to do was stay.

You fell for me *too early,*
and I fell for you *too late.*

MY FIRST LOVE (STAY BEAUTIFUL)

4/23/19
3:24 pm

Corey,
we were friends,
but I saw you as more than that.
But don't worry,
all my feelings are in the past.
We've grown and changed
in so many ways.
Sometimes I wonder if it's for the better.
I'm not so sure these days,
at least when it comes to me.
Do you ever think about me
and the time we spent together
playing on the trampoline,
eating crackers in the back seat
as you rode home with me,
or when we played
dress-up at my house?
You wore my heels
and a dress, and I laughed
like it was the funniest thing I'd ever seen,
because perhaps it was at the time.
You made me so happy, so full of joy.
You were my favorite boy.
Did you know I had a crush on you? I'm certain you had to.
You meant everything to me,
but did I mean anything to you?

My mom and I went through photos
the other day.
We kept a Christmas card from your mom.
You guys were down by the lake
with your golden retriever,
a lovely family photo that
now makes me so sorrowful.
It's been hard for me, too,
but for you,
I imagine the grief was hefty,
unbearable even.
And I'm so sorry I wasn't there
to help you carry the weight
of losing so much
before you were ever an adult.
I don't know how you did it,
how you survived it all.
You've been so strong
when you shouldn't have needed to be.
I drive by your old house
and I recall the days
that the bushes out front were finally trimmed
and no longer hung over the street.
I went to school and mentioned it to a friend,
and he had noticed too.
So perhaps I'm not the only one
with you on my mind.
And I hate that we lost touch,
that I don't know what happened to you
when you left,
where you moved to.

I'm sure that house held
too many memories for you,
because it does the same for me.

Every time I drive by that house
I think of you.
I can't even fathom
the hell you've been through.
But you look happy now,
at least in the pictures I've seen.
Is she good to you?
Did she comfort you in ways I never got to?

We were best friends once upon a time,
at least I considered us to be.
I still remember the things you were allergic to,
the things that made you smile,
the bands you listened to.
I can't listen to Green Day without thinking of you
and picturing your face,
perhaps that's because Billie Joe's eyes
remind me of yours.
The dark outlines on such light eyes,
you were such a sight for sore eyes.

I sung along to "Stay Beautiful"
because in my mind
Taylor was singing about you.
Your eyes are like a jungle;
I could get lost in the blueness of them,
like a ship in the ocean.

I still think about you from time to time,
and I pray to God you're alright.
And I worry about you
more often than I ought to.
I remember growing up
always seeing your father's truck driving down the road.

I wonder what ever happened to it,
the custom license plate
from his arborist business.

Corey, I envy your strength,
your tenacity.
I've admired you
since we were young,
and I hope you know how greatly
you're loved.
I loved you, too, once upon a time,
back when I didn't know what love was.
I've loved you in many different ways,
as a friend, as a crush,
but now I'm certain I've always loved you
like a brother.
You're so strong,
and I'm sure many people have told you that.
And perhaps you're sick of hearing it,
because you might not feel that way.
But look at you,
after everything, still intact.

You'll always be the beautiful blue-eyed boy
who stole my heart.
Before I ever knew the meaning of love,
I knew I loved you.
I wish you the best,
and I pray you'll find the peace you're owed,
the happiness you deserve,
and a love that will last your whole life.
You're beautiful;
every little detail is admirable.

Don't you know that
you're destined for great things?
Just ask anyone,
they know it's true.
And when you find all that you've looked for,
all you deserve,
I hope you're led back
to my front door.
But if you aren't,
stay beautiful.

SCINTILLATE

8/13/18
1:07 pm

Sparkles,
glitter,
tears.
All shine
at midnight
in moonlight
on the drive home
after drinking away your fears.
Your makeup rolls down your face
as you cry away your troubled day.

The glitter on your dress cannot
distract from the brokenness within your chest.
Your tears rest upon your cheeks and glimmer
in the neon lights.
You beg for someone,
anyone,
to ask you what's wrong.
But no one does.
No one ever does.
Just once you want someone to care.
You thought that guy at the bar cared
until he stuck his hand up your dress
and began to aggress and undress
you like all you were
was bone and flesh.

Everyone took all you had
to offer, and you gave it away
willingly.
The emptiness inside you couldn't be filled
with the liquor in a shot glass, but still,
you tried.
You thought he would help you
feel alive,
feel loved,
feel something,
anything.
And all it left you
feeling was empty.
You found love and fulfillment in a boy
who never wanted to take you home.
All boys do is cum and go,
that's what you told me.
All you really wanted
was to be loved
by someone,
anyone.
You cried out for help and no one
seemed to listen.
You cut yourself open
and tore yourself apart,
begging for attention that your parents never gave.
You went home every weekend
sneaking back into your bedroom
in your mother's house,
regretting everything you'd done
while you were downtown.

Then you did your best to wash out
the scent of liquor from your blouse.
I don't know where you are now or how you're doing,
but I hope you're better than you were senior year.
And I hope you know that you deserve more than
just a one-night stand with some mediocre man.
I know you've never felt love in this life.
I know how cruel they've been to you.
I know you've wanted it all just to go away
so you try anything to fill the void.
Believe me, I understand.
You thought alcohol would drown out your sorrows,
but it only amplified them.
You thought drugs would help you forget,
but the amnesia was only temporary.
You thought boys would fill the emptiness inside you,
but they only left you feeling unsatisfied and used.
To whoever you might be,
and the one whom I know specifically,
I hope you found your way,
and I hope you no longer
feel the need to rely on outward things to validate you.
No high can make your troubles go away.
No liquor can wash away your pain.
No high will make you feel okay.
When you're sober again,
and the sex is done,
and the drugs have worn off,
you will be alone again.
Your emptiness can only be filled by one thing.
A single void with one solution,
a savior to rescue you from the depths of misery.
There's someone who has what you've been searching for.

The cure —
love, comfort, security,
an overwhelming sense of belonging.

One in three,
there is an answer for you and me,
immaculately incarnate
solemnly sworn
to trade transgressions
hand in hand.
An uneven trade,
the unfairness of grace we can't earn,
no matter how hard we try.
With profound acceptance,
there's a revelation within,
beginning and spreading outward
like wildflowers.
It grows in places without hope,
once desolate spaces now lay aglow.

Sparkles,
glitter,
tears.
All shine
at midnight
in moonlight
as you release your fears
and trust in the one who has put you here.

YOU WOULD LOOK SO PRETTY IN A PRISON CELL

11/2/18
11:07 pm

Today my mother met a girl who was raped by you.
Was she just one of many?
Could I have been your next victim,
another conquest, another girl defiled by you?
I thought I knew you.
Now I wish I never did.
How could you do something like this?
But I don't feel bad for you, not a single bit.
I feel bad for the girl you assaulted.
Did you think about the repercussions
of your actions and how they would affect
her for the rest of her life?

This was just another pit stop for you
on your path of destruction.

Did you even know her name?
Did you realize that your actions would
ruin her life and make her want to die?
I can't believe I once called you my friend;
now I don't even consider you an acquaintance.

To think you'd force yourself on someone unwilling
makes me feel sick to my stomach,
but at the same time, I'm unsurprised
that you'd do such a thing.

The way you made so many girls uncomfortable,
begging for nudes, then apologizing,
saying it was someone else on your phone.
But we weren't stupid… we knew,
and we were disgusted by you.

You always used force,
any tactic you thought would work.

And it's not lost on me
why you've always reminded me of my father.
Like him, you're a monster,
capable of manipulation and destruction.
I don't know the full story,
but I don't need to
because I know you.

To the girl he assaulted,
I wish I could take away all of your pain.
And if my attempts were unsuccessful,
I'd erase your memories from that night,
with your permission.
I'd sever his hands off if I could,
I'd do just about anything to get justice for you.
I wish I could write you a happy ending
so you'd know all the pain you went through
wasn't for nothing.

But I'm incapable of such things, and some days
I'm not sure pain has a purpose beyond making us ache.
I truly hope that isn't the case.
So I hope you find a way to live and be content
in spite of him.

WHERE'S MY JOURNAL?

I had the words perfectly recited last night.
At 3:04 AM, as I tossed and turned in bed,
the words were perfectly arranged in my head.
I swore that I would remember them
and write them down in the morning.
I committed them to memory
while everyone else was asleep.
And I awoke without recollection
of what felt like an innovative creation at 3 AM.
I knew I had words to write,
but they had slipped from my mind,
and I was so sad to have lost them.
They were so powerful.
There was a sense of urgency to them;
they needed to be shared.
But I guess they were just meant for me.

FORGOTTEN POEMS AND DREAMS

11/6/18
8:04 pm

Dedicated to:
All of the emotive poems I've crafted
in the middle of the night
that I never had a chance to write.

In remembrance of:
All of the beautiful dreams I forgot
immediately after waking up,
despite how desperately I tried to cling to them.

The worst part is,
it's always the best poems
that come to my mind at 2:00 AM
that I can never remember in the morning.
It's always the sweetest dreams
that evade my memory so quickly,
the ones I want to live in
for even a moment more.

And it's never fair
how my mind clings to the things
that I wish I could forget.

JOVIAL

Happiness greets you once again.
Her familiar smile reminds you of an old friend.
Her embrace will warm you and remind you
why you persisted despite everything
the world threw your way.
She walks with you through a valley of vibrant
flowers illuminated
by the brightest sunlight.
She shields your eyes with her right hand
as she grips your hand tightly with the other.

You escape her grasp
as the void of darkness
threatens to take you back.

She whispers to you,
"Be still in this moment.
Embrace everything surrounding you."
You focus on the feeling of your feet
beneath you, holding you up.
You notice your poor posture and roll your shoulders back,
now sitting tall with your head
angled upward, facing the sky.
The sun meets your face like a gentle kiss,
spreading warmth across your skin.
The mountains in the distance are covered with snow
and the trees on either side of you
are abundant with the sweetest smelling fruit.

The sunlight dances off the tall grass
as it sways by your feet.
You close your eyes as you reach
your hands to the sky.
You walk forward with confidence
in just the sway of your hips.
You run through the grass and wildflowers
in awe of all the delight this world has to offer.
You fall back onto the soft pillow of grass
and lie back to watch the clouds pass by
as you decipher what each one looks like.
The birds sing a melodious song
as the wind whistles along.
You throw your hands to your side
as your fingers brush against
the dewy blades of grass
extending to reach your palms,
and you can't help but laugh.
The happiness you are feeling
is overwhelming you.
You roll onto your stomach,
wondering how this could be.
Why me? you ponder.
"This is too beautiful to be seen by just me,"
you scoff in disbelief to Happiness.
Your eyebrows furrow as she
bends down to meet your gaze
and whispers, "You deserve it."

And I sit for a moment
as silence hangs in the air between us.

Tears begin to well in my eyes,
because I find her words too good to be true.
She grips my wrist, pulling me up from where I lay.
But how could this be?
I don't deserve to be this happy.
I deserve pain and sadness,
like I've always had.
Happiness lifts your face
with confusion in her eyes
as she shakes her head from side to side.
"You do not deserve pain.
You've been through enough.
You have come from the void;
you are not destined to stay there forever.
You are in a land where only contentment may reside.
No pain can permeate, no worry is welcome,
and you will be received with open arms
anytime you visit."
"Visit?" you ask as your smile sinks into a frown.
"I can't stay?"
Happiness explains,
"I'm sorry, my love, it doesn't work that way.
Pain is inevitable, but it isn't deserved.
It demands to be felt,
which is why you cannot stay here.
But in the void, you can think of me and remember
these feelings and know that you can feel them again.
You're not permitted to stay here indefinitely,
but you can take a piece of me with you."
She reaches down and plucks a flower from the root.
"Take this with you, plant it, and watch it bloom.
Contentment can exist even in the darkness."
You smile softly and nod your head, thanking her silently.

"This is the Jovial land
where light is impermeable by darkness.
But in the void of Gloom,
darkness can be overcome by light."
In the Jovial land, contentment cannot be touched,
but it can coexist with darkness in Gloom.
Happiness hangs her head and looks down
at the emerald grass beneath her feet.
She sighs and meets your eyes once again.
"I wish you could stay, but you must go.
You can only stay a few minutes more."
I hold her hand tightly in mine.
"This isn't goodbye. It's simply 'see you later.'"
I will see Happiness again soon,
and I'll take her contentment and plant it,
thoroughly watering the roots,
and soon enough I'll have my
dose of contentment too.
If I must traverse the valley of pain,
then I will bravely trek through,
because I know I will experience
spots of contentment throughout.
And Happiness will be waiting for me
at the end, so long as I carry on.
I know I can persist because
even though pain is a void,
I have the strength to climb out
with the moments of joy and clarity
provided by the flower Happiness gave me.
Soon there will be a field of flowers
overtaking Gloom, leading me back to you.
I must go through all of this
to once again hold the hand of Happiness.

CHANGE, IT'S LONG OVERDUE

11/9/18
9:21 pm

Is this what America has come to?
School shootings and bloody tributes —
another mass shooting took place this week.
It's become routine.
It feels like they happen more and more,
and as the seasons begin to fade,
the wearier we grow.
Are we just numb to the pain?
Are we used to the calamity in our headlines,
unfazed by the number of casualties in our cities?
As I read the news on my feed,
I cry and feel weak in my knees.
And I wish thoughts and prayers could do something.
We need change;
it's long overdue.
How many more need to die
until people realize this is an issue?
How many more teachers must sacrifice
their lives so their students don't have to?
Why must it be this way, constantly fearing for our lives?
There must be something in the air
making us immune to these tragedies.

These mass calamities are not just bruises
that need time to heal,
they are wounds that leave everlasting scars...

On communities.
Families.
Friends.

Every body.
Are guns more important than people?
At this point, that's how it seems.
These killers are running wild and free
just waiting for the next opportunity.
The constant fear for our lives
has become normal to us.
They want to get us used to the idea
of this kind of death.
But we will not stay silent.
People are dying every day
because others aren't willing
to sacrifice their guns for human lives.
We need to stop waiting for the right time —
the right time is now.
We need to make it stop.
Kids shouldn't fear going to school,
and we shouldn't expect another mass shooting,
but still, we do.
We shouldn't fear for our lives
every time we leave the house.
People are more important than guns.
Every single life is important and valuable.
Maybe it's time we started acting *as if that were true.*

BEAUTY EXISTS IN EVERY SHADE OF MELANIN

I've never understood how someone
could look at another and determine
their value based on their skin tone.

Every person is beautiful and worthy
of life and love, regardless of their skin color.

Dark,
light,
or in-between,
doesn't matter;
they're all beautiful to me.

It's what's inside that counts.
I want to know the person,
the soul beneath.

DEVASTATION

With a pained expression,
he mutters, "Goodbye."

And behind his tear-filled eyes,
I see a fire slowly dying.

At that moment,
I knew it was our last goodbye.

MAGNIFIED

She grips her tears and hides them
by her side so no one can see
the way she grieves
and how badly
she wants to slip
away from existence.

She hides her insecurities
behind alcohol and clothes,
hoping that some boy will
want to take her home.
But they were never enough
to fill the emptiness inside.

The pain in her chest still radiated
late at night.
When the high subsided and reality set in,
she was alone…
again.

BREAKING GIRL-CODE

What would she do
if she knew
I loved you too?

Lauren Hope Bartling

HE FELL TOO SOON

I had a boyfriend in the fifth grade.
He was new to our school,
and all the girls liked him.
I didn't understand what love was then,
but based on my limited knowledge, I concluded
I was in it.
I thought I loved him,
but I was too young
to believe I knew what love was.

Even now, I'm unsure
I know what love is.

But you liked me,
which only proved to complicate things.

I was a child, young and tender.
He made my heart flutter
and brought sunshine into my life.
He didn't talk much, but that was alright.
To this day, I still think of him,
my first case of infatuation.
And I still find myself drawn
to people who resemble him.

I can't remember much about my brief relationship.
It felt like it lasted a year when it was
probably only a couple of months.

But I recall bringing him candy
in hopes of him still liking me,
a feeble attempt at gaining another's affection,
as if chocolate was enough
to keep someone interested.

My father did the same thing,
giving gifts. After an argument,
he'd show up with flowers for my mother
and a bottle of champagne.

I wonder if that's the reason I'm so good
at gift-giving.

But I prefer to think I'm observant,
empathetic,
that my gifts are evidence of my affections
rather than pleas for theirs.

I had two boyfriends in grade five.
Both were sweet, but neither alike.
And then there was you…
the unspoken number three,
who could've had my heart…
my everything.

I loved as much and as deeply
as the definition of love that
11-year-old me could carry.
So why did you have to ruin it for me?

I remember the pain when he broke up with me,
devastation unlike any I'd felt before.
And I never got a reason why.
It was so sudden, out of the blue.
And for a girl who thought she knew love,
she then thought she knew grief too.

The next school year, I was talking to Corey
in the library when we were meant to be reading.
He was one of my first crushes,
a dear friend of mine,
who I still think about from time to time.
I don't remember how the conversation started
or who brought it up,
but he told me
you were the reason
he broke up with me.

You told him to break up with me.

You told him to dump me,
and he had someone else
deliver the message to me.

I know we were only children,
but my emotions were still real to me then.

And I don't resent you for what you did;
I just wish you had been brave enough
to tell me the reason.

And I know it's petty to hold something against you
that happened over a decade ago,
and I promise I don't.
It's just another page in our story that
I must divulge to help make sense of it all.

A pivotal point in our timeline where you liked me
before I liked you —
a classic case of *he fell too soon.*

And I know it's all so silly and elementary,
but at the time, I was heartbroken and angry.
I saw it as a malicious act
with ill intent, aiming to hurt me.
Now I see it for what it was:
jealousy.

Still, I wish you had just talked to me
and admitted your feelings.
I wish you could've been honest with me
Maybe our story would've ended differently...

A LOVE LETTER TO THE OCEAN

I miss your
      salty kisses
          and the way you made me feel
   a little unsteady when you held me.

I miss the way you made
      me feel everything
  and *nothing*.

I miss your embrace
    around my waist.
        The way you made me feel alive,
     as if I existed
        exactly where I needed to be.

I hope to be with
    you again soon.
       But I know
  you're always
     waiting for me.

COULD YOU LOVE ME AGAIN?

8/18/18
11:28 pm

The lake always reminded me of you.
I was sitting in the back of a boat
while waves splashed upon my face
as I passed your house, and I wondered
what could have been
and if I would have made you happy back then.
I imagine what it'd be like
to sit on your lap and feel your arms
around my body, holding me.
I envision us by the shoreline,
spending hours talking,
not noticing the passage of time,
and soon enough it's twilight,
and you'd invite me to stay the night.

And I craft a life together in my mind,
just to watch it slip away into the sand,
another effect of my delusions.

To this day, I'm uncertain
I know what true love feels like.
But I know you were the one
my soul felt drawn to.
I feel like I lost my chance with you,
the person who could've been the only man
to ever hold my entire heart in his hands.

We fit together like two pieces of a puzzle,
but as we got older, our edges began to crumble.
In every person I see, I envision you
and pick out the features you share.
And I try not to compare,
but it's hard not to
when it's you.

I felt like I knew you as if you
were a part of me,
intricately woven into my being,
but perhaps that was merely my hope projecting.
I admire every aspect of you —
there is not a single facet of you
that I do not find fascinating.
The way you made me laugh,
your contagious smile,
the way you listened and understood me,
the way you loved me, even unromantically.
It was never romantic between you and me,
but there was chemistry
threatening to overtake us,
that neither of us dared to confess,
so we stayed apart,
never to undress our feelings,
leaving our affections fleeting.

The connection between us was
tangible and undeniable.
Still, I tried so hard to deny it,
and I did a good job of it,
because I lost you in the process
of learning I loved you.

We were best friends as children, so close
I believed you would've chosen me,
but to my surprise,
I wasn't even in your top three.
I was an accompanying party in the back seat,
lost in the crowd of people who adored you.
Did you know I adored you too?
I begged and pleaded with God for you
to reach out, but you never did.
And I still have your number
but I'm too scared to call it.
Because what would I do if you picked up,
or even worse, if you didn't?
What if you changed your number,
or went rogue and completely ditched
the digital world?
How am I to know
when I don't know you anymore?

We used to sing songs by Queen on the playground,
and you used to tease me.

God, you were such a pain in the ass.

You hated it when I called you by your first name
rather than the middle name you went by.
I loved to see the way you rolled your eyes —
you'd get so annoyed, and that felt like a feat to me.

Was I like another sister to you
or something undefined?

Did you like me?
Is that why you got jealous when you found out
about my crush on your friend?
Is that why you got up and made fun of it
in front of everyone?
Did you not want to see me
happy unless it was with you?
Then why didn't you try
to make your wish come true?
You never made any grand gestures,
no confession of love, so what did you want?
Because if you wanted me…you should've told me.

Did you love me?
Because I think I loved you.
I'm not sure if I still do,
but deep down there will always be
a part of me
that is still holding onto
the dream of having you.

I grew older, and so did you.
That's when you met her.
She was perfect, an ideal match.
You two were the couple cliché
in a romantic teen movie.
She was a cheerleader,
and you were on the football team.
I hated seeing you two together.
I didn't know why until now.
It was because I wished she was me.
I wanted to be the one
you went to school dances with.

I wanted to be the one
to hold your hand.
I wanted to be your first
and only love.
So call me jealous, call me selfish
because I wanted you
all to myself.
But you fell *too soon*,
and I fell *too late*.

It was our senior year, and we
hadn't talked in a few years.
You grew taller and stronger; you looked so good.
You finally cut your messy blond hair.

And I believe I owe you an apology,
so I'm sorry for being cruel to you.
I'm sorry for pushing you away.
I'm sorry for saying those words
I never meant to say.
I hope you can forgive me one day.
I tried to convince you
that I hated you.
I told you I did too.
And it breaks my heart now to think that you
thought that was the truth.
I'm sorry for making you believe that lie,
because the truth is
I could never hate you.
I think it was easier for me
to push you away
than to watch you leave me.

And I didn't want to be the one
left in your dust,
so I made you choke on mine.

I couldn't face my feelings.
I knew that you were with her and I
had to move on.
I didn't want to hold you back.
I wanted you to be happy,
even if it wasn't with me.
I pushed you away when all
I wanted was for you to stay.
I wish I had known that sooner,
but now it's too late.
You've outgrown me.

I told myself you were the only person
I could ever imagine marrying.

We grew up together.
I saw you in every phase, every stage.
To be with you would be so simple.
But I don't think simple will suffice
for me in this life.

Your name will forever be
engraved at the top of my heart.
You were always there,
from the very start.

We're in college now, and you live in a different state.

It took me so long to realize
the only reason I like him
is because he reminds me of you.
Everything about him,
from the way he smiles
to the way he walks.
But he doesn't do it quite like you.

The way your eyes crinkle when you smile,
how your eyes light up when you look at me.

Please don't forget me.
Go…and be.

We're older and you're no longer
sober. You've changed so much.
You are not the boy I used to know,
and you're not much of a man, either.
You're going to frat parties while I stay home
and watch old TV shows alone.

I will always wonder what could have happened,
but I'm content never knowing.

You deserve only the best
this world has to offer and nothing less.

I love you… in the most platonic sense.

And I hope you know that you are the one
thing in my life that got away
that I'd gladly take back.

GO AND BE

The only boy who ever really swept me off my feet...
not in a romantic way, at least not initially.
Rather, in a way that showed he truly cared about me.
I always saw him as a friend.
For as long as I can remember, he was there,
him and his messy hair.
That's how I'll always remember him.

I wish I had realized sooner
that you were everything I wanted.
You were my best friend at one time.
We might not have always been close
but you were the one who always understood me.
You were always so kind to me
even when I tried to convince you
to stay away from me.
I was afraid that I would ruin your reputation
if you were seen with me.
I don't know why I told you I hated you.
I don't know why I said you were mean to me
when you were only ever kind.
I wish I could go back in time
and change it all so we could be friends again.

Maybe then
you would've stayed.

It wasn't until you began to appear in my dreams
that I realized just how much you meant to me.
At first, I just saw an old friend.
Then I saw something more,
a future, with you.
And the sight was frightening and delightful
all at the same time.
Being with you felt right,
and we were happy.
That was the day I knew that I loved you,
even if it was *fleeting* and *momentary*,
unrequited and *small*,
the feelings were present.
I don't know if I still love you,
but I know a part of me did
and always will.
And I hope that at one point
you loved me too.

A LOVE LIKE OURS WOULD'VE PUT
MOVIES TO SHAME (USED TO BE)

I dreamt of him weekly,
or at least who he used to be.
I dreamt of the idea of him,
and what we could be.
But now he's just a frat boy
partying in Mississippi.
He's gained a bit of weight,
and his hair has turned a bit darker
than it used to be.
He isn't the boy I used to know
and love. And he never will be.
I fell in love with the idea of him,
who he used to be,
what we used to be.

I still have dreams of him,
but not like how they used to be.

HE DIDN'T EVEN KNOW ME

6/16/18
1:47 pm

I'd rather live with the fear
of never knowing
what could have been,
than live with the knowledge
that he didn't want me in the end.

But which is worse?

I guess I'll never know,
because I'm too scared to find out
but too afraid to let go.

DON'T ROMANTICIZE THESE THINGS

6/21/18
8:55 pm

Mental illnesses are not adjectives
used to describe how you're feeling.
Panic attacks are more than stage fright
and nerves before an exam.
Panic attacks are ugly and brutal;
they take everything out of you.
As I stood in my bathroom tonight,
my entire body shook.
All I wanted was for it to stop,
but it wouldn't.
There was nothing I,
or anyone else, could do.
Feeling sick to my stomach,
I slumped over in pain and watched
as my knees trembled beneath me
uncontrollably.
My body was shaking violently,
my breathing was rapid and labored,
and my vision blurred.
My body felt weak and tired
from trying to calm down
when it simply couldn't.
All you can do is wait.
So, impatiently, you wait
for the shaking to stop,
for the dizziness to subside,
for the nausea to disappear.

After all, all you've got is time.
Time to question everything.
Why me?
Why this?
And you'll find no answers to these questions.
You stand quivering in fear
at your own body attacking itself
and you simply want to understand why.
Why?
I tried to pray it away,
but no remedies were found on my knees,
only my hunched back over a toilet seat.
They say patience is a virtue,
but I lose all my mine
when my body is stuck in fight-or-flight.
My body is drenched in sweat
when the shaking finally ceases,
then I collapse, exhausted, and cry.
It's a never-ending cycle.
It's vicious and hungry,
the illnesses that reside inside me.
Unchosen and unwanted,
I have no choice
but to endure them.
Something given and received is not guaranteed
to be selected and esteemed.
Often there's no say in the matter,
only managing.
Regardless of the burdens given,
We still carry them.
So our shoulders ache and our necks hurt
from the weight of symptoms and diagnoses,
prescriptions and coping mechanisms.

No one would ask to hold such heavy things
so don't tell me I carry these ailments willingly,
as if they are not the result of trauma inflicted on me.
Don't tell me to pray it away
or go outside and get some solar rays —
"That'll surely take all the mental illness away."
But if there's no choice given
there's no option to have it taken away.
Instead, it's something you learn to live with,
a permanent nuisance.
And it may ebb and flow.
With the changing seasons
it's sure to shrink and grow
but it's always there,
a screw poking through the carpet
waiting to torment you;
a sensitive car alarm
that rings with a gust of wind.
There's no changing the body I was born in;
there's no removing the PTSD.
My generalized anxiety and panic disorders,
my depression and complex trauma,
my emetophobia and disordered eating habits
are all intricately woven into me,
something I cannot erase or ignore.
And there's absolutely nothing
quirky about my anxiety
and the trauma-induced panic attacks I've had.
There's no idealistic aspect of it.
It's exhausting living in a body that's fearful of everything
so I can't understand how people
use these terms so carelessly.

Obsessively they clean so they claim
to have a compulsive disorder,
when they just prefer things tidy.
Even my father wrote off my diagnoses,
each one he disregarded.
He even had the temerity to claim
he experienced the same things,
anything to shine the spotlight on him.

Mental illnesses are not enviable.
They take a toll on you and your entire being;
every facet of you is impacted.
I encourage a conversation on such topics
so long as it's not stigmatizing and toxic.
So feel free to hang your dirty laundry up with me.
Let's share therapy notes and stories
of daddy issues.
Don't romanticize these things.
Don't use somebody's everyday battle
as an adjective for a fleeting feeling.
Be respectful of the gravity of these topics.
Mental illness is not cinematic or beautiful
like it's been portrayed in television and movies.
It's raw
and it's real
and it's deadly.

WAS IT ALL IN MY MIND?

6/15/18

I sit on a boat
admiring a bright blue sky
when a cloud slowly creeps over me.
Rain and lightning stir above me,
heavy and loud.
I shiver as the storm worsens
and thunder begins to strike.
The waves crash
upon the side of the boat
making my stomach flip
around inside me.
I begin to feel seasick,
with a sense of impending doom.
The storm now seems to expand
across the entire sky with no end in sight.
I sit down in the corner of the ship
the storm had tossed me in and cry.
My soul feels detached from my body
as I watch my limbs tremble uncontrollably.
I'm frozen.
I cannot move.
This is the end,
once again.
My heart thumps louder and faster.
I grip my hair in my hands
and cry out my last goodbyes.

I look to the sky to determine
just how much time I have left,
but when I look,
I see nothing but clear skies.
I am completely dry.
Not a cloud in sight.

Was it all in my mind?
Could I have simply imagined it?
But...
there was a storm,
I saw it with my own eyes.
But where did it go?
How am I completely dry?

I stood up, still woozy from what just happened.
I gripped onto the side of the boat as my knees
buckled underneath the weight of my body.
My legs were still slightly trembling
and my chest felt tight.
I tossed my head back and sighed.
There was never a storm.
It was all in my mind.

But the dangers seemed real at the time.

PROZAC

6/14/17
11:40 am

My anxiety struck again.
What a familiar feeling this is,
to feel as though I'm drowning
in my own thoughts.
I cannot quiet my mind no matter how hard I try.
My brain is going a million miles a minute
with no end in sight.
The intrusive thoughts
come in waves as I push them away,
feeling disgusted with myself once again.
I try to calm myself,
but nothing seems to work.
I cannot take this anymore.
I want to cry and scream
but I'm afraid if I do,
I might never stop.
This weight on my shoulders
is much too heavy for me to carry alone.
It's all too much,
existing has become overwhelming.
The neighbor mowing the lawn next door
becomes a siren suffocating me.
Every sound suddenly intensified
as my heart begins to thump
irregularly inside my chest.

The worries take over
my thoughts as I begin to hyperventilate
and shake uncontrollably.
My vision blurs as I begin to feel dizzy.
I sit down on the floor, unable to think
of anything other than the seemingly
approaching doom.
My stomach starts to gurgle
as the physical symptoms start.
Nausea and sweat,
fear and regret.
Unable to calm
down, I move to my bed
and watch the time
pass on my alarm clock,
waiting for the agony to cease.
I pray
and I pray
and I pray,
but the prayers don't help me.
I then worry what God thinks of me,
then I fall asleep,
aching and depleted.

LET THERE BE MORE

10/19/18

Crying on my bathroom floor
praying for something more,
more than this pain and heartbreak,
all I've ever known.

Why did they leave me?
Was I not good enough?
Was I too much?

Because of you, I became accustomed
to the idea that people would hurt me,
leave me.

You made me think I wasn't enough.
It's all because of you.
The pain I bear inside my chest
has your name engraved on it.

But you can never own up to what you've done.

So I sit here with emptiness inside my soul,
longing for what I've never known,
what I'll never know.

You were supposed to be the one person
who was always there for me.
You were supposed to love me.

You convinced me it was all my fault,
the harsh divide between us.
But how was it my fault that you didn't care enough?
You did the bare minimum at everything you did,
never enough, only ever grazing the surface.

Why was the responsibility on me?
It wasn't my job to love you,
It was your job to love me.

Sure, you said those three words
but they were empty sounds coming from you,
with no purpose,
no meaning,
no value.

Was I too much?

Because of you, I became accustomed
to the idea that people would hurt me,
leave me.

You made me think I wasn't enough.
It's all because of you.
The pain I bear inside my chest
has your name engraved on it.

But you can never own up to what you've done.

So I sit here with emptiness inside my soul,
longing for what I've never known,
what I'll never know.

You were supposed to be the one person
who was always there for me.
You were supposed to love me.
You convinced me it was all my fault,
the harsh divide between us.
But how was it my fault that you didn't care enough?
You did the bare minimum at everything you did,
never enough, only ever grazing the surface.

Why was the responsibility on me?
It wasn't my job to love you,
It was your job to love me.

Sure, you said those three words
but they were empty sounds coming from you,
with no purpose,
no meaning,
no value.

LETTERS TO ME

11/2/18
12:24 am

You will be okay.

Tell yourself this
as many times as you need
to truly believe it
and know that in the end
you will be okay.

Maybe not today.
But someday you will.

Somehow.
Some way.
You will be okay.

ROSE-COLORED LIES

1/2/15
11:18 am

I need someone to fix me,
I need someone to take away the pain,
But oh, darling,
I know I can't change.

A HISTORY OF TAKING CARE OF YOU

I know life is so confusing and challenging,
but please keep fighting.

Your life has so much value and meaning.
You are so full of light and love.
This world needs you here.
So stay
and live
and love
and flourish.
Grow and become
all that I know you can be
and more.

You are so beautiful,
deep down to your soul.

You may feel lost and confused,
but someone is guiding you through
this life and holds a greater purpose for you.

It's okay to not know what to do;
there's no pressure,
no rush.
Take your time;
your best is
and will always be
good enough.

Take some time
to breathe,
to live,
to do,
to be.

Be completely and utterly you.

I've stood where you now stand,
walked those same roads,
and cried the same tears.
I've felt the same fears,
that keep you up at night,
wondering what will happen in five years.

I know what it feels like
to want to give up;
it seems like the better option
than to continue
staring into your half-empty cup.

But you've come so far,
you've fought so hard.

And somehow,
you always make it through.

So remember
in the valleys of life
what you've been through
and know
that God has a history
of taking care of you.

CAPTIVITY

11/7/18
8:20 pm

We all have fears in this life,
but you don't have to let them control you,
no matter how hard they try to.

How to do this...
I wish I knew.

FRAYED

Be still in this moment.
Your anxieties do not define you.
Your sadness will not linger forever.
Trust me,
you will make it through this,
because I did too.

Be still and know
you'll be alright, even if it feels like
your whole world is crumbling.

It's okay to cry,
to scream,
to ask why.

Please know this season will pass...
just like all the other ones have.

You are here for a reason.
Your pain will not last forever.
You will make it through.

You are welcome here.
Your brokenness,
all of you,
is wholly acceptable.

We need you.

THE DEFINITION OF GRACE

your
past
mistakes
and
yesterdays
do
not
define
who
you
are
today.

REMEMBER THE TRUTH

I have to constantly remind myself
that what is true in the light
is also true in the dark.

When the skies are gray
and my soul feels heavy
I must remind myself
that the sunlight will surely come again.

There are bound to be dark days
that feel never-ending.

But they *will* end,
and the sun *will* rise again.

No storm can consume you.
You may emerge drenched and sullen,
but sunlight will soothe your tired bones.

It may take time,
but the night always ends
with a sunrise.

I'M SORRY I APOLOGIZE TOO MUCH

I said sorry as if it was as vital as breathing.
And to this day I still do.
I apologized for everything —
from broken plates
to wrinkled lines in my clothing.
I apologized for the way I felt
and after every single word I would say.
I always thought people were mad at me.
I thought my presence was an annoyance,
an inconvenience.
I doubted my likability.
My anxiety told me they'd leave anyway,
so I pushed them away
before they could
even contemplate leaving.
I knew they wouldn't stay,
and it hurt less
to say goodbye this way.
I was always too something —
too clingy, too needy, too… me.

I'm sorry for pushing you away.
I'm sorry for being a burden.
I'm sorry for making you angry.
I'm sorry for being me.
I'm sorry for saying sorry.
I'm sorry for everything.
And I'm sorry I can't write
what isn't true.
I'm sorry I only write things that are dark and blue.
I'm sorry I can't be who you wanted me to be.
I'm sorry.

I FEEL FAR TOO MANY THINGS

Where does my anxiety stop
and where do I begin?

It seems as though I'm ninety percent fear
and only ten percent who I used to be.

WHAT DOES MY FUTURE HOLD?
DO I EVEN WANT TO KNOW?

5/23/18
2:04 pm

I lie in my bed staring at my ceiling
waiting for my thoughts to quiet.
My chest tightens as the voices inside
echo things I don't want to hear.

> *No one will ever love you.*
> *You're not good enough.*
> *You're pathetic.*

I cry as the words resonate.
They ring true in my head,
and I want to be swallowed whole
by my bed.

I roll onto my side and wonder if they're lies —
they seemed true at the time.
I look at the empty right side of my bed
and wonder if the voices are right.

> *You'll never get married.*
> *No one in their right mind*
> *would ever want to be with you.*
> *You would be a horrible wife*
> *and an even worse mother.*

The voices of my doubts and fears
have my voice, but it's higher pitched,
grating, ringing in my head.
I can't quiet them.
I try to shake them away, but they won't go.
They've taken residence in me
and changed their address permanently.

I flip onto my back and look up
at the ceiling once again
as my mind is racing with possibilities,
things that might not occur.

And it breaks my heart
to have such high hopes
and to be the one
required to quell them.

Will I be alone in five years?
Ten?
Will I be content even then?

Will someone ever truly love me?
It's been ingrained in me
that people only ever leave.
But could someone come into my life
and rewrite that narrative for me?

What if I'm unequivocally not enough,
and worse, what if I never get the chance to find out?

I don't know who to believe,
me or my anxiety.

HISTORY OF HEARTACHE

When I was falling apart at the seams
I didn't want someone to stitch me back up,
I just wanted someone to grip my torn edges
and tell me that it's okay to feel this way.

Still, my brokenness felt like a burden at the time.

So I tried my best to pray it away,
and I cursed myself when it didn't work.
Perhaps if my faith were stronger
I wouldn't be suffering.
If only I believed the right amount,
I wouldn't be deserving of such afflictions.

I cut my skin open,
hoping that bleeding would help me
feel something.

And I suppose it did;
it made me feel worse…
shame…
the need to hide something
behind long sleeves and Band-Aids
at only 15.

I pretended I was fine at the time.
I had to maintain my composure,
a good girl from a good family.

I could be an actress,
the way they believed me,
that I was perfectly fine…
It's sickening, honestly.

Inside I was slowly fading away,
dying internally,
never externally,
never showing my wounds,
never letting them see
the worst parts of me.

A steady life
on the outside.

A rich neighborhood,
emerald green grass.
I always had a pass,
an excuse,
a reason,
why I shouldn't be sad.

But I had every justification
for the persistent ache
in the form of my dad.

Everyone thought I was exaggerating,
a teenage girl couldn't possibly know suffering.

They thought I was playing pretend,
a game of aching,
like it was fun
to make-believe my anguish.

I never faked anything…
except maybe contentment.
And I never realized my pain could be felt
by another, not until
I was at the doctor's office with my mother.
It was my first of many,
a mental health screening,
checking boxes
picking the amount of time I'd felt certain things,
like the tendency to harm myself
or the urgency to end everything.
She cried in disbelief in the grocery store parking lot
before she went in to pick up my new prescription.
She grabbed my hands and looked at my wrists,
wondering how I turned into this.

And I felt like I had been reduced to a speck
in this vast universe.
A spot circling a black hole,
a blemish amongst nothingness.
A tarnishing of humanity,
a stain on creation.

A mistake of a girl,
a mess of a child.

I wept in the car
as I tried to explain my pain,
but every explanation fell short.
No words could encompass the feelings engulfing me.
So I resorted to displaying it on myself,
a physical manifestation
of inward turmoil.

But I grew past that.
I stopped tearing at my skin
and realized there was a better option.
Hitting walls.
Because a tiny cut wasn't enough.
I needed to ache,
I needed to bruise.
I needed something that would last,
that would ache longer
than the bleeding.

I needed to hurt.
And I needed to hurt externally,
no longer just internally —
an expression of my self-hatred.

I'd always find a way to hurt,
to make myself ache,
because it's all I've known,
so I feel deserving.

And if I'm not aching,
I must not be living,
so I inflict pain upon myself
as evidence of my existence,
or perhaps a repercussion of it,
a consequence.
It's what I'm owed.

It makes me feel more human,
to have control over the ways in which I suffer,
the method by which I ache.

To destroy myself on my own terms
feels more innate.

Perhaps when they see me tattered and unwell,
they'll spare me an ounce of empathy,
and they'll finally believe me.

I'm an anxiety-ridden girl
who fears I annoy another
with a mere word
and worries others will choose to leave
instead of love me.

So I cause myself pain,
because perhaps it's easier that way,
to be so well acquainted with ache
that I'm numb to its sting.

And when another comes along and tries to hurt me
I'll be immune.
At least that's what I tell myself,
but I know it's not true.

I may be jaded to my core,
but I'm gentle.
So gentle, in fact,
that a mere strong breeze
is enough to make me tremble,
for I am so fragile
that my heart will burst
a millionth time
the same way it did the first.

And I think that's an equally tragic
and beautiful quality I hold,
to have become so scarred
but still contain the ability
to bleed, to have a heart
that's been broken
yet still able to beat.

And I don't deserve to hurt,
I never have,
I never will.

I've known enough pain
to become soft,
not calloused;
not cold,
but tender
and warm.

I've hit the right side of my hand
hard enough against wooden doors
that it went numb and couldn't bend.

It still hurts to this day...
the aftermath of rage.

And the bruise lingered for a month,
purple and green,
my resentment towards me,
my enablement of my own suffering.

I only wanted my pain to be seen,
to be felt,
to be acknowledged.

My scars are ornaments on my being,
reminding me of all I've traversed through,
and I wouldn't dare to have them covered up
or removed.

My journey is far from over
and my aching will linger,
but I refuse to participate
in the production of my pain.

I won't further my aching;
I've known enough suffering.
I'm a cockroach of a girl,
refusing to give in,
surviving the worst of things.
I've become a warrior,
a gentle one,
because when struck
I still bleed,
despite everything,
despite the history
of my heart aching.

DON'T PLAY THE VICTIM

Why did you expect me
to respect you
after all the years of neglect
you put me through?

GRANDPA'S GONE

Death is such a confusing thing to me.

One day you can be full of life,
and the next,
gone.

I don't think you can ever get over someone's death.
It feels surreal.
Existence alone is such a monstrous concept —
too big to even begin to comprehend.
The absence of someone feels so
strange that you doubt if it's real.
Sometimes, you sense them here
as if they never left —
like it was just some sort of nightmare.
The memories come rushing back,
making you nostalgic
for the past and wishing you could go back
and say "I love you"
one last time,
or apologize for that silly argument you had,
or even just hear their voice
one last time.

Their presence is now a distant memory
that you long to feel again.
But you have hope, knowing they're in a better place
watching over you and
saying the *I love you's* that you forgot to.

REBELLION CAUSES DISTASTE

11/19/18

I have run away.
And suffering from my stubbornness
cannot be so easily erased.

My soul feels so empty; it needs to be fed.
I need just a drop, but my taste buds are dead.

What I need, this world cannot provide.
The food of this earth cannot satiate.
What I need is you, Lord,
to come and take away this pain.

Forgive me for running away
and forgetting all the promises you've made.

Lord, feed my soul,
let my tongue experience
the sweetness of your love and grace.

2014 AND LIVING IN THE EMO SCENE

The cuts in my heart
are longer and wider
than the ones in my jeans.

That's what you did to me.

You broke me down
and left me there
to wither away.

Does it give you some type of twisted pleasure
to hurt those who once loved you?

How could you hurt me like that?
Don't you know scars can't be fixed by Band-Aids?

You move on to your next victim
without a second glance in my direction.

You took all I could give,
offering nothing in return.

And I know you'll do the same to another,
and I won't be able to warn them,
because I'll be too busy mending my wounds
to stop you from causing more bloodshed.

And I'll blame myself,
like I always do.

POLAROIDS OF THE PAST

As I dug through my drawers
my hands came across something
foreign and unfamiliar.

It was an old bag, stuffed full.
I dumped it out onto my bed
and out fell Polaroids from years ago.
I had hidden them away,
out of sight, out of mind, so they say.

I took the faded pictures
and scattered them across my bed,
and as the memories flooded back, I began to cry.

Pictures of the memories we made,
Halloween parties and Tumblr grunge days.
You were my best friend,
always there for me when I needed you most.
You promised me you would never leave me…
so why did you?
You left me and all the memories we made behind,
abruptly and without reason.

I took the tear-drenched Polaroids
I'd been reminiscing over
and cut them into pieces.

And to this day I hate that I threw
our treasured memories away.

OVERANALYZE

I hide beneath the guise that I'm fine,
while I overanalyze every little sigh —
the fault must be mine.

HE REMAINS BESIDE ME

6/8/18

My depressive tendencies
begin to take hold
of the better parts of me.
They tell me I'm not good enough.
They ask me why I even bother trying.

My chest sinks as the words ring true.
The sadness eats at my insides
and tears me apart at the seams.

I cannot be sewn back together, not again.

This time I've been ripped too far,
tugged on too roughly.

The threads sit at my sides
as I frantically try to sew them back together.
But as I sew one side, the other begins to unravel
again. It's a vicious cycle

of putting myself back together
just to fall apart all over again.

I gather all the threads
from my torn-up vessel
and set them in my hands in front of me.

Examining my brokenness under a microscope,
I begin to cry into my palms,
and the threads begin to shrink.

I let out a small gasp as the threads
begin to dance in front of me,
slowly stitching themselves back together.
Seam by seam,
they begin to sew me back together.

They pull at my sides
as they pull me up
and straighten me out.
The threads intertwine with my flesh
and make me whole again.

The sorrow, sadness, and shame I've felt
have turned into my saving grace.

My brokenness has been made whole once again.

As the final short bit of thread
ties itself into a knot,
a sigh of relief escapes my mouth,
and I collapse onto the floor.

I lay on my back and gently raise my arms,
examining myself, the patchwork of my parts.

I never thought I would see myself in this form again.
It had been so long, I had forgotten what it felt like.
I had been made new.
But it wasn't the tears that saved me;
there was no magic within them.
It was the power within my weaknesses
that saved me.

I cried out to God for help.

He orchestrated the seams of my being back together.
He built up new walls and put me back together
with silver string, tough but delicate enough for me.
He stitched together the gaping wounds of my soul.

He saved me.
He made me whole.

He saw potential in me.
When all I could see were pieces,
He saw me entirely.

And He puts me back together,
again and again,
with nothing on His face
but an enamored grin.

TOO YOUNG TO BLEED

At only the age of 17,
my heart had been broken
and scattered one too many times.
I'd been torn apart at the seams,
Too young for so many heartbreaks.
Too young to bleed.

And it always lingers…
the ache of missing another.

But sometimes people leave,
people change.
People will hurt you and walk away
without a second glance your way.

They will rip your heart out
of your chest and tear it open
in front of your eyes,
watching for your reaction.

Tears stream down your face,
wishing,
hoping for something better,
something more.
Unfazed, they turn away.

Now you're left to grieve…
to grieve the presence of someone you once adored,
someone you've now come to abhor.

ROOM 219

Let the laughter consume your soul,
reminding you that you're alive to feel.

This planet you were put on
was made to be seen
and experienced by you.

Those butterflies fluttering
in your stomach,
making your heart beat
a million miles an hour,
are proof that you are a miracle.

Alive.
Breathing.
Living.

This beautiful life is your own.
Enjoy every single bit, wholeheartedly.

Go and enjoy it.

Watch movies with friends
and stay up till 3 AM
talking about frivolous things.

Lauren Hope Bartling

Enjoy the little things in life,
the beautiful sunset dripped
with saturated golden and peach tones
or the flower patch on the side of the road
that grew in between spaces of concrete.

Don't be afraid to put yourself out there,
try new things, and go places you've never been.

Laugh until your stomach hurts
and cry till you can't anymore.

You're alive…
and you're alive to feel things,
good and bad.

Let the positive and negative
things consume you.

Allow yourself to drown
in your sorrow and
float on your happiness.

SUFFICIENT

10/30/18
11:11 pm

I wish,
at this moment,
for you to stay alive.

You are worthy of so much
more than you think.
You are worthy of breathing
and living
and existing.

This world needs you so much.
You make a difference.
You matter.

Please don't give up.

I know it feels like the only option.
And I know you've tried
so hard
for so long
to simply survive.

But please don't die.

You are important to so many people.
Your life holds value and meaning.
Your thoughts and feelings
do not determine your value.
You are worth every beautiful thing.

You are so full of light and love.
I know you want to die, and at one point so did I.

But please, stay alive.

You don't need to be perfect or "fine" all the time.
Being you is enough.
And you are beautiful…
you are worthy of life and love.

You are strong and capable of pushing through.
So, please… don't give up.

Please stay alive.

If you are looking for a sign,
this is it.

You are alive for a reason,
a purpose,
that involves,
requires,
you.

You will feel alive again, in time.
I know you just want to feel something —
anything.
So be patient and know
that there is something better waiting for you.

And remember... you are never alone.

MINDFULNESS

Even amid the storm you are facing,
you are going to be okay.

Because at the end of every storm,
at the last drop of rain,
sunlight
will once again show her face.

Her beauty will illuminate
your day and remind you
that it's okay
not to be okay.

Because, in the end,
there will always be sunshine,
even after the stormiest of days.

THIS ISN'T THE END

Your life will feel
as though
it is ending many times.

But that's okay,
because it's just *an* ending,
not *the end.*

You can fall apart and not die.
I know because I have many times.

CAR CRASH

All the kids in the neighborhood want to die.
We're all sad and falling apart inside.
Our minds are being terrorized
with doubts and worries that can't
seem to be quieted with any drug or high.

All the kids want the pain to go away.
But even in their dreams,
they see nightmares
of having to live another eternity.

All the kids want to feel something
so they do anything to just feel again.
They take every pill until
they pass out in the kitchen.
They try and try but no escape
can keep them away
from reality long enough.

All the kids want to do is feel alive.
They don't want to die;
they just want to numb the pain.

But it's okay to feel all these things.
Remember, this is not the end.
Your pain will cease,
and you will feel happiness again.
So dive into the depths of your despair,
but know that you will not stay there.

MASQUERADE:
I'M DONE PLAYING PRETEND

Everything looks perfect on the outside.
But inside, this house is filled with lies
and a pillow full of tears I've cried.
The walls cannot forget the words
that were yelled down these halls.
The door still has trouble shutting
after being slammed one too many times.
The corner still has blood from my right knuckle
after I punched it last December.
I just wanted to feel something.
To hurt.
To bleed.
So he could see how much he hurt me.
But he only laughed and turned away.

This house isn't as bright
as it used to be when I was a child.
All I see now is a house full of broken memories.
The family dinner that winter
when he was drunk and slurring his words.
The Christmas he argued
and made me cry till I couldn't eat.
He asked what was wrong with me,
but never assumed the answer was him.
I guess he couldn't see
that I wanted to die,
that I was in so much pain inside.
We went to the theater, but I couldn't make it in the door.
I ran to the bathroom, refusing to go in.

I cried in the stall for an hour,
trying to muffle the sound.

But they didn't even notice anything was wrong.
The panic attack I had in that restroom still haunts me.
I can never look at that stall the same.
I wanted to die.
The anxiety was too much,
and the newfound depression wasn't helping.

But nobody understood.
They didn't want to.
My mother didn't even notice.

And I can't erase the scars I've carved
into the sides of my wrists and fingers.
I was in a black hole and people tried
to convince me it was all in my mind.
And it was; that was the problem.
I had no physical evidence
of my mental suffering,
so I tried to create some.

I am a shell of the girl I used to be.
But now, somehow…

the sun shines a little brighter
and my mind is a bit tougher,
refined from agony
that was once seasonal
but now is perpetual.
And the picket-fence houses
look perfect on the outside,

but on the inside, the wallpaper is melting off
and there is no one there to notice
the little girl crying alone in her bedroom.

They don't want to see what happens
in this house when no one is around.

But I saw everything.

I apologize for ruining your perfect
manipulated perfection, Dad,
but you were never the man
you portrayed yourself to be.
You never even tried to be.

And as your house was falling apart,
you sat back and watched.
You turned the volume up,
enjoying being the witness,
the catalyst,
to our downfall
while you were drowning yourself in alcohol.

I was exhausted after trying to be
your perfect doll for so long.
Now everyone knows that your home is crumbling.

And I am so much better than you will ever be.
Not because I'm perfect...
but because I don't pretend to be.

NIGHTMARE

He made the shadows less scary,
because he was the monster
looming in my closet,
haunting me each night
as I tried to sleep.

WINTER AIR

I went to the cemetery where he was buried
for the first time in almost six years.

I didn't think much of it until I was there.

The thought that all those stones
had people beneath them
who once lived and breathed
terrified me.

Then when I found your gravestone
I felt as though I couldn't breathe.
The tears fell out of my eyes
and down to my side,
reminding me of the pain and misery
that had become so familiar to me.

I wondered how people did this in the movies —
they made it look so easy.
But I couldn't stay.
I had nothing left to say.
He wasn't here anymore
and pretending he was
made me hurt that much more.
I couldn't sit there and talk
to who you used to be.
You aren't there anymore.
All being there did for me
was bring back sad memories.

AM I STILL ME IN THE MIDST OF UNCERTAINTY?

I'm still waiting for my purpose.
Will it ever find me?
I need to know what to do.
I look in the mirror, but
my reflection doesn't look
quite the same as it used to.
I'm older.
Sadder.
Confused.
I stare at myself,
thoughts running through my head.
What is my purpose?
Would I rather be dead?
No,
I tell myself and shake my head.
I rub my eyes and try to quiet my mind.
But it's no use
because the voices inside
can't be put on mute.
I look back at my reflection,
my stare unwavering,
and the colors begin to fade and blend
as I sink into the wall behind me.
My silhouette becomes unclear
as my vision blurs and the colors
in the room continue to smear.

I stretch my hand to the mirror
to try and make it stop.
My eyes follow my hand
back down to my side
then I look up again and see myself.
Not a random person.
Not an image that had become distorted.
I saw myself.
Someone whom I had yet to know fully.
I tell myself I know who I am,
but as I look in the mirror
at the person in front of me,
I wonder,
is this the person that I want to be?
I clench my jaw and furrow my eyebrows
as tears cascade down my face.

What is wrong with me?
Why can't I just be happy?
I just want to know what to do.
I want someone to tell me.
I want someone to give me
an instruction manual for living.

I don't know who I want to be.
But this girl in the mirror,
she isn't me.
She's pretending.

I feel so uninspired and sick and tired
of pursuing something that only makes me want to retire.

I deserve happiness.
I deserve love.
I deserve every wonderful thing from above.
I tell myself I need to make up my mind,
but I remind myself I still have so much time.
But my mind is too indecisive,
and I'm too lost to even know what the options are.

I'm so far behind,
I'm still on the opposite side of the finish line,
watching others pass me by.

I want to be myself
and not who someone else says I should be.
I am me.
But I don't even know who I am.
I am me.
But who am I?
I am anxiety.
I am worry.
I am fear.
I am doubt.
I am uncertainty.
But I am here.
I am present.
I can make up my mind,
and change it again in time.

What do I want to do?
I wish I knew.
I'm so afraid of failure that I don't even try.
Instead, I do something else
and put all my hopes and dreams aside.
Waiting for the right time.
But there is no right time.
There never will be.
There is only here and now.

MOOD SWINGS

7/21/18
4:30 pm

From incredibly happy one minute
to completely falling apart the next.
Why must life be this way?
Why can't there ever be a happy medium?

It's one extreme or the other.
I'm not strong enough
to keep fighting this war inside me.
I feel so alone,
yet this anxiety inside my chest
clings tightly to me.

The fear of everything
and nothing
weighs heavy inside me.
Every morning I'm greeted with reality,
I try to make the most of it
and force a smile.
Then, when night falls, darkness comes.

And it comes to haunt,
to bring out the worst in me.
The moonlight greets my gloom
with a bittersweet kiss.
I try to quiet the fear that exists,
but nothing works.

My body trembles, and I cry out
of sadness and exhaustion.
My head falls onto a tear-soaked pillow,
desperate for sleep,
for some sort of escape from this perpetual ache.

WHY I WRITE

6/21/16
1:16 pm

Writing, to me, is a form of escape.
I can make real-life tragedies into art.
I can turn chaos into creativity.

I write about horrible situations,
allowing them to come to life
by turning them into poetry.

They're not beautiful things,
so I don't write them to be.
They're hellish endeavors
that become ornamental works.

But blood can only ever be blood.
No matter how you describe it —
rich and flowing,
maroon and glowing.

That blood loss was never once alluring,
        it was only blood.

And my pain will remain the same,
only ever heartache and anguish,
never once poetic.

I write these things
knowing it won't change the reality of them,
but in hopes that I'll find peace
in the worst situations.

I don't care who my writing inspires
or depresses, because I don't
write to please or comfort them.

I write for me.
And that's the end of this story.

I read a quote once
that art should comfort the disturbed
and disturb the comfortable.
And that is exactly what I aim to do.

My secret hideaway exists
between the present and the words that slip
onto a keyboard from my fingertips.
I type the words endlessly,
feeling them flow out of me.
Letters pour out, turning into words.

It's a form of therapy.
It's my escape from a world
that is far too cruel
for a tender thing like me.

LEFT ON READ

I'm
single
and
content
so
please
stop
texting
me,
I'm
spent.

ILLUMINATE

I write selfishly,
all for me.

I write about him
in hopes of finding peace.

I cannot write only of love,
miracles, and happiness.

I have brokenness inside me
that begs to be seen.
I am so completely vulnerable,
even behind a computer screen.

My walls have been built up so high
that I can't even reach the top.

But I also hold an abundance of love inside.

I hate to see others in pain,
even when I feel like I'm dying inside.

My soul is full of gardens that overgrow
into others' lives and flourish amongst my own.

My mind is full of complexities,
like a ball of yarn, impossible to untangle.

But even then, I still see it as my friend.
And I fall to my knees
crying and begging,
please take this away from me.

The weight of existence
is too much to carry.

This light inside me
can only shine so bright in the wintertime.

And it will blow out from time to time.

But spring will come
and thaw out the parts of me
that had frozen
and reignite the light inside my eyes.

And this, too, I will write.

Although I carry this light inside,
sometimes it doesn't shine as brightly.
But even then, my stories are worth telling.

The lights come and go,
as do my positive emotions,
with the snow.

And yet my words are still powerful
and clear throughout the year.

They might be melodramatic and depressing,
but so am I before the coming of spring.

And that is the way it will always be.

So read my poetry
and appreciate it all,
because they are all parts of me,
the good,
the bad,
and everything in between.

My poems are like life
and all its many sides,
and they so desperately want to be seen.

Just like me.

WHAT IS IT LIKE TO BE FREE?

You said it was hard to live with me.
And with that,
I completely agree.

COMPOSITION NOTEBOOK

You are in my DNA —
that I can't change.

You've forever made a mark on me,
scarred and bruised,
aching and used.

But I won't let
the things you've done
define me.

I might not be who you wanted me to be,
but I'm more than enough for me.

8:53 A.M.

I sat there and cried in her arms for an hour.

The nightmares of you now haunt me nightly,
and the fear has transposed into my waking life.

So I was left weeping in a high school bathroom
while you never had a clue.

You were guilty
in the eyes of everyone
but you.

And I won't let you off easy.
You won't have the final say,
not after everything I've seen.

Not after becoming the product
of your misdeeds.
I won't let your conscience sleep.

If my dreams must be haunted by you,
your memory will be riddled
with curses from me,
tormenting, truth-telling.

SHE HELD SO MUCH LOVE IN HER HEART...UNTIL HE TORE IT APART

"He really is a terrible person
To mistreat two beautiful women like you.
He never deserved to be loved by you,
Especially after all he put you through."

UNREACHABLE

I wanted to be
loved
by a man incapable of
loving.

UNRECOGNIZABLE

She said she hated going home to see him.
I told her to treat him like a stranger.
She said, "He already is one."

APATHETIC

3/16/19
10:01 pm

I told you what you had to do,
You said it was too hard for you.

To fight,
To stay,
To be better,
To change,

To love me in a way
That didn't leave us estranged.

LISTEN FOR ONCE

I cried and fell apart
in front of your very eyes,
and all you did was ask me why.

As I explained everything,
all you did was gaslight and lie,
turning productive conversations
into circular ramblings.

Could you have
just listened for once,
maybe?

DO YOU REGRET ANYTHING?

Today I realized I no longer want you.

I had spent so much time trying
to be enough for you, trying
to make up for the lack of love you showed me.

But today was my final realization
that I don't want you in my life anyway.

You would never be able to give me what I wanted,
what I needed.

And nothing you say
could erase all the years
you abandoned me.

Today I declare my independence from you,
and in my heart, I've moved away.

All trying has left me with
is years of yearning and hoping
only to be left discontented.

But now that you're gone, I have to be honest,
I still miss you on occasion, but I'm better off for it.

And I hate to wonder —
Is being content without you a sin?

CIRCLES

Resolution
in our conversations
could never be reached.
Maybe it's because
our relationship
had already been breached.

THE ONLY PERSON WHO LOVES YOU IS YOU

He bragged
about all the women
he flirted with
but could never get.

GIRL ERASED

We argued for hours that Saturday afternoon,
and you told me how all I did
was never enough for you
because it wasn't what you wanted me to do.

I wasn't interested in the things you thought I should be,
and you always held that over me.
Maybe if I did what you wanted me to
you would've cared about me
the way you cared about him.

You asked how you hurt me,
and I listed all the ways,
but you didn't bother to listen.

"He was always your favorite,"
the words spilled from my mouth.

But you didn't even respond.
You didn't even deny
the allegations; maybe because you knew
they were true.

You would bend over backwards
to please him in any way.
You loved him more than me,
and you rubbed it in my face.

Parents aren't supposed to have favorites,
but mine did, and it wasn't me.

He never saw me the same way
he saw my brother.
He treasured him.
Or perhaps he pitied him.
When he looked at me, he saw all the things
I could be — ought to be —
rather than who I was and all I aspired to be.

The years I spent doing what I loved
never made him proud;
they only made his anger grow.

I would never be enough for him.
To him, I would always be a disgrace.

His words are lies
and his eyes
full of deceit and despise.

He never saw me for all that I am
and all I plan to be.

And I'm going to become someone
he will never get to meet.

IT'S TOO LATE

I needed a father in the past,
but I never got that.

I never had his approval,
his guidance,
his love.

And it left me feeling incomplete.

He can't make up for all the years he wasn't there.

But now I know I don't need him anymore.
What I need now is to realize
that my worth doesn't reside in him,
and it never did to begin with.

I don't need his approval or guidance.
And although I needed his love,
I can live without it.

BUT THAT WAS TOO DIFFICULT FOR YOU

"I lost my job. What was I supposed to do?"
he yells at me from across the room.

I shut my eyes tightly
as I let out a heavy sigh.
My jaw clenches as I try to refrain.

But I'm unable to stay quiet,
not again,
never again.

I take a deep breath and say,
"Your job was to stay."

But now it's too late,
and I wouldn't want you back anyway.

ATHLETICS

You were only proud of me
when I did something you wanted me to.

Otherwise,
I was nothing but a disappointment to you.

Lauren Hope Bartling

FINE CHINA

I stood beneath the scorching water
from my shower as the light of three candles
danced around the room,
glowing on my pale skin.

The room steadily filled
with heavy steam
from the water stream.

I scrubbed my skin as hard as I could,
trying to erase the marks you left on me.

But it wasn't that easy.
The scars you left me with weren't skin deep,
they lingered inside my bones
and rang throughout my being.

I stood there quietly
as music hummed all around me.
I stretched my neck to the ceiling
as my hair fell past my waist.

I couldn't seem to wash away
all the years of history between you and me.

But I tried and tried
that Saturday night
to empty myself of what you had left in me.

As the water shut off
I was left with my thoughts again,
alone, yet content in the silence that surrounded me.

The candlelight began to fade
as I focused on the steam coming from my body.

I ached from the boiling water
I bathed in to try to erase
the marks you left on me.

I couldn't even look at you
without my hands shaking
and my heart palpitating.

The fear of who you could be,
who you had been,
and what you had done to me.

My legs began to tremble as I thought of you again,
so I shook my head trying to get you out,
and I steadied my legs beneath to obey me.

As I took a deep breath and slowly exhaled,
I blew out the candles.

And with one final breath,
I extinguished the final hold you had on me.

You are nothing but another chapter of my history.

DIPSOMANIAC

I no longer recognize you.

I try to not linger too long on your eyes
because they are the only honest part of you.

I can so easily see behind your mask
how you're falling apart inside.

Is that why you drank?

Did it help take the pain away?

I guess it did
because I haven't seen you
since that day.

I suppose I was the cause of your ache,
the way you're the cause of mine.

Like father, like daughter.
I'm only a leaf from your vine.

PAINTED IN PAIN

You critiqued me
the whole way home
that night.

It was hard to drive
with tear-filled eyes,
but you didn't seem to care.

You never apologized
for causing all the tears
I've cried.

But I guess it's okay.
At least the crash was on your side.

WAS IT WORTH IT?

He called me boring because
I didn't want to do ecstasy.

He said I didn't know how to have fun
because I never tripped on acid.

But he could never take just one to feel relief,
he had to take three.

And he couldn't convince me
his lifestyle was superior
as his smile sat slack and inauthentic.

He felt bad for me
because I wasn't living
the way he was at 17.

But it was him I felt bad for,
because he had to alter
his natural state to enjoy living.

He was alone in his own world,
so desperately wanting to be seen.

And drugs just aren't for me;
the addiction in my bloodline is unforgiving.

I know the feelings may seem tempting,
the temporary relief that's only ever fleeting,
never lingering,
never healing,
never fixing.

Drugs are fun
until they aren't.

And addiction isn't pretty —
there's no such thing as heroin chic.

I've seen parents lose their children
and children watch their parents
become shells of themselves
because what they wanted most
was on the top shelf
or in an orange bottle.

There's nothing fun about watching a person wither away
or having to administer naloxone on a first date.

There's no such thing as California sober.
This isn't a fence you can sit on;
you're either on
or you're off.

THE FIRST CHRISTMAS WITHOUT YOU

Tired eyes
And heavy sighs
Filled the air
That late December night

ELEMENTARY

My mind can't seem to erase
the memory of you,
no matter how hard I try to.

I thought I saw you in the supermarket today.
My heart fluttered at the thought of seeing you again.

But it wasn't you.
It never is.

I tried to leave you in the past.
I tried to forget you.
But my subconscious won't allow me to.
I go weeks without thinking of you
until you show up in my dreams unannounced.
And I'm pissed off you live in my head
when I wanted the real thing instead.

My heart has always longed for you.
Ever since the first day I met you,
I knew there was something special about you.
I remember that day
with clarity and vividness unlike any other.

I was only 5 at the time,
but I still recall the day you came into my world,
you and your messy blond curls.

I don't know why, but all my oldest memories involve you.
You are etched into me.

But now,
I think I'm just
in love with the memories.

Maybe we will meet again
a few years down the road
and we can try again.

Maybe then
we could be
more than friends.

SANITIZER

His presence was enough to sicken me.

His clothes reeked of the cigars he had been smoking.
He'd try to cover the scent
with mints and scented
hand sanitizer, but they were only masking agents.

They couldn't get rid of the stench.
The smell of mediocrity and a middle-aged crisis.

Smoking marijuana and drinking absinthe.
Living like a frat boy,
trying to recreate his glory days
that he'd brag about at parties.

His breath stunk of the liquor
he drank in the early morning.

His eyes were empty of all but his fears.

His soul was barren,
his heart, incapable of loving.

That's why everyone left him.

And why once they were released from his shackles,
they'd sing a hymn of freedom and solidarity,
worshiping the distance now between
and trying to cope with the harsh memories.

YOU SAID YOU LOVED ME,
AND I WISH I BELIEVED YOU

I was a failure in your eyes
because I didn't follow
the path you wanted me to.

I'm not sorry to tell you this,
but I'm the happiest I've ever been
without you guiding my hand.

You hoped I'd do what you never could,
but our dreams were different.

You couldn't accept my ambitions.

You crushed every one of my hopes and dreams
before I ever turned 13.

But watch and see me bloom
into all I was destined to be.

You always underestimated the intricacies inside me.

Where you saw a delusional little girl,
I saw a vision of a powerful woman,
created from the hell you put me through.

And I will achieve everything I've set out to do
without you.

HEART OF STONE

Why can't you be happy for me?
Why can't you see that isn't who I want to be?
Why can't you accept me for me?
Why was I never enough for you?
Why can't you let me do what I want to?
Why are you so cruel?
Why did you hurt me... endlessly... needlessly?

And how could you not see
the effect your words had on me?

You broke me.
Tormented me.
Crushed me.
Relentlessly.
Unapologetically.

Why must your heart of stone
beat my tender heart black and blue?

What must I do to make myself lovable to you?

MAMA

I could write
a whole book
about you.

But there would never be
enough pages
to portray
my love for you.

I'M SORRY

Sorry I disappointed you.

Actually, I'm not.

But I do apologize for not living up to
your expectations of me,
ones that you yourself could never meet.

I'm sorry that you could never be proud of me.
I'm sorry that you felt the need to control me.
I'm sorry I wasn't enough for you.

But mostly,
I'm sorry on your behalf,
because you missed out on knowing me.

Instead, you tried to create
a version of me that didn't exist,
an idealized version of me you wished
was reality.

And I can't blame you for that,
because I did the same thing with you.

The only difference is who I am
is far better than who you were.

Only my fantasy of you
could compare to the reality of me.

RESERVATION

his love had boundaries and standards
that I could never meet
his love was conditional
and never for me

GASLIGHTING

You made me doubt my sanity.
You made me think you never really hurt me.

I fell for your lies,
time after time.

But never again
will I let you in.

I didn't imagine
being hurt by you.

You just can't admit to yourself
that the reflection you love so deeply
can also be hated by so many.

You made me who I am today
not by influence,
but through pain.

I stand a strong woman today
because I never allowed you
to get in my way.

WILL YOU BLOCK OUT HER WORDS TOO?

she had to scream to be heard
but even then
they didn't bother
listening to a single word.

— the story of a woman begging to be believed

AVERAGELY ME

7/17/19
8:52 pm

I never felt as faulty as I did that July night.
Not a single picture turned out right.
To the left,
to the right,
not one angle was able to satisfy.
My hairline appeared crooked
and my face looked bloated.
Every picture was blurred,
my self-image distorted.
As I walked the aisles of the supermarket,
it felt like all eyes were on me,
and not for good reason.
I felt their unsaid words cut into me.
My sunburnt skin was already tinged
with pain, but their stares
only added to the ache.
And perhaps I was reading more into it
than there was.
But at the time I could've sworn
everyone looking at me
was thinking the same thing.
They were thinking about how atrocious I looked,
pointing out my flaws in their heads,
like I had done from the moment I got out of bed.
These beautiful girls passed me,
and I gripped my stomach and side-eyed
my frizzy hair.

God, I wanted to disappear.
I walked by a sunglasses stand
and my reflection caught my eye.
It wasn't a pretty sight.
My stomach turned as I was reminded of its size.
But no amount of sucking in would make it go away,
so I use my arms as a distraction,
covering the larger parts of me.
My thighs,
my hips,
my stomach with one too many rolls on it.
My lips remain small,
but they have big goals.
I gripped my sides
and looked down as I walked
through the aisle of
supermodels on magazine covers.
Oh, how I wish
I were invisible in moments like these.
And what makes it worse
is the likelihood that nobody even noticed me.
Everyone was probably caught up in their thoughts,
ruminating on their own self-perceived flaws.
A stranger's words couldn't hurt
more than the thoughts running through my head.
I hate myself more than I'd like to admit.
I try so hard to love myself.
I fake confidence I've never felt.
But all I see when I look in the mirror
are the things that make me unworthy,
unlovable, and unseemly.
I never see myself for more than parts of a whole,
and maybe, for once, I'd like to admire my sum.

WHO ARE YOU?

I don't hate you; I hate what you put me through.

IF I SHALL DIE

7/27/19
12:59 pm

If I die before publication,
please ensure my voice is heard.
Please ensure my work is seen.
My words must be spoken
so everyone can see how vividly I'm hurt.

If I die before I see success,
please let them know that I wish them the best.
Please tell my mom I love her so much,
and that she deserves happiness away from him.

If I die, send me away and out of sight.
Bury my ashes deep below the ground
where I can never be found.
In my childhood backyard is where I wish to rest,
lay me there so I can be at home once more.
Sing me away with a song of escapism,
and remind me that there will be better days.

Don't let that vile man shed a single tear over me —
all he did was torment me.
He is not welcome here.
He doesn't get to mourn me.
Please let me go and know this is for the best —
I no longer have pain inside my ribs.

Mom, I will show you
the beauty in this earth
that seems dead.
Every rainbow above your head
will be me softly singing of hope and peace.
Please get the rest you deserve,
and know that you don't owe him a single word.
If my lungs give out and my heart stops beating,
please remember me for the better seasons.
Remember the way I smiled and the way I laughed,
remember me for all of that.
I wish not to die,
but to see a revival on this side.
To see success firsthand
and know what it's like
to get away from that man.

Lord, let me survive another day,
another night,
and keep her at my side.
Let us see what it feels like
to have peace and happiness.

We beg for a way out of this war zone;
please give us the happiness
we've been longing for.
Please keep me alive
to see my work come to life.

I want to see it with my own eyes,
the impact I have on others.
I know I would be a good wife
and an excellent mother.
I will keep fighting this war,
but I won't keep score,
not anymore.
God, get us far away from him,
and let us feel true freedom.

If I shall die before I wake
I pray the Lord my soul to take.
If I shall wake instead, then I shall pray
and thank God for giving me another day.

END GUN VIOLENCE

When did guns become more valuable than lives?
Then again, maybe they've always been in this nation.
How many more people need to die
for someone to realize this isn't right?
How much longer until something is done,
or will they just wait until there are
only the people they agree with under the sun?

FAMILY GATHERING

My heart is so full and content today.
The smile on my face cannot be erased.
But then it hits me.
The day is over,
And I have to go back home,
To him,
Again.
The trauma never ends.
After two perfect days with chosen family,
I have to go back to reality
And the hell I was born into.
        A loveless home.
Sometimes I wish
This feeling would last forever,
But it never does.
Reality hits
As soon as I walk through the front door.
Sadness fills the air
With the memories of previous arguments
Etched into the walls.
But his day of reckoning will come
And collect him and leave him with nothing,
Not even phone calls.
One day the happiness I feel today
Will not be a momentary thing,
But an everyday occurrence.
And after all I've been through, I deserve it.

YOU BROKE MY HEART

Didn't they tell you not to hurt a writer?
I guess not,
because now you get to see what happens
when you break a writer's heart.
They will use every word to reveal
exactly how you tore them apart.

GET OUT OF JAIL FREE CARDS
DON'T EXIST

9/18/19
6:22 pm

You stabbed me in the back
then placed the knife in my hand.
You told me it was my fault I was bleeding.
"Look what you've done," you said to me.
"You did this to yourself, can't you see?"
With tear-filled eyes, I said my goodbyes.
I took the knife out of my back
and collapsed on the ground,
still clutching your weapon in my hand.
I lay on the bloodstained carpet
in a room full of despair.
You lied to me so many times —
didn't you know I could see it in your eyes?

You hurt me for the last time.
You don't get to pretend everything is fine.
You don't get an apology for my blood on your hands.
The fault will always lie with you.
I stitched myself back together one last time.
I packed my bags in the dead of night,
when you were asleep and unable to stop me.
I left before sunrise and flew
the farthest a couple hundred bucks would take me.
I tossed my bloody shirt in the garbage can as I left,
with the knife you stabbed into me, and
five inches of hair I cut off at the kitchen sink.

Enough evidence to frame you for the death of me.
But is it really a frame job
when you were the perpetrator all along?
I ended up at Myrtle Beach with a brunette bob
and a cheap pair of sunnies.
I walked into the ocean fully clothed,
looking completely insane,
because perhaps I was.
Besides, all that's left of me
is the aftermath of you.
So I sank beneath the water,
letting it cascade over me
and fill my lungs.
And I drank up the sea
and felt my body being
pummeled against the ocean floor.

And for once I didn't mind the pain,
because you weren't the one inflicting it.
I scrubbed my arms with sand,
trying to wash away the invisible marks you left on me.
The salty water burned as it hit where your blade had been,
but I reveled in the sting
and watched as my blood tainted the water around me.
I laughed at the sight of me bleeding out around tourists,
because you never allowed me to ache publicly.
That was only something I could do privately.
I was only ever allowed to suffer silently.
But now I get to display my wounds
and give tours of my scars.
The scars that will linger forever
are all I have left of you.
No memories of happy times.

You could never take responsibility for all you did to me.
It's not my fault you forgot to love me.
Did you forget how to love?
Or perhaps you never learned how to.
Either way, there's no excuse.
It's too late for you.
I've given you a million chances to come through,
and every time you remind me why I didn't want you to.

So I stopped trying,
but not before you.

You stopped trying long before
I felt the responsibility to.
You thought it was my duty to love you.
But I was just a child;
my devotion wasn't owed to you.
You were the one who was supposed to love me
unconditionally,
but you were never there for me.

Now all I have left from you are scars and wounds to clean.
My scars still bleed,
but I no longer see you in them,
I see me.

I see the person you made me.

A violent vision of a woman who never got to be young.
A girl thrust into war, with no way out.
A girl who only wanted your love.
A girl who felt like she was never enough.
A girl heartbroken and hurting.

Your knife will never dare touch me again.
My walls stand sturdy and tall.
And I swear my heart will never love again,
because you said you loved me,
and if that's what love is,
I want nothing of it.

NARCISSIST

10/02/19
10:59 am

Break my heart,
I dare you.
Hurt me with all you've got.
Just know you'll get caught.
Everyone will know what you did,
because I turn all my pain into poetry.
So enjoy the chapters all about you.
I'm sure you'll love them.
After all, your favorite topic is you.

"FAKE IT TILL YOU MAKE IT" DOESN'T WORK WHEN IT COMES TO YOU

7/21/19
1:14 pm

Every time I start to see something positive in you,
your true colors shine right through.
Your anger and hatred cannot be covered
by your facade of faultlessness.
Every time I give you a chance, you remind me
why I needed to stop giving them in the first place.
All you do is break my heart
and tell me your faults are mine.

You told me I ruined everything, but it was you
and that damn cabernet.
My words were too convicting, so you disregarded them.
You said I took away all your joy and happiness that day.

Go ahead, call me the devil then throw me away,
just another average Tuesday.
You villainize me for the crimes you commit.
You apologized, but it was never sincere.
You'll never be sorry; that much is clear.
I was looking for things in you that were never there.
You'll never be what I need, much to my despair.

DO I DESERVE TO HURT?

What am I without you?
I fear that I'm nothing more
than a sore
from a bad seed of yours.

I fear being around you, but I fear leaving you more.

Who will I be once I'm set free?
Will the fear still haunt me?
All I've ever known are your cold touch and silent words.
How will I part from all the things I've never heard?

I feel this pull towards you,
telling me I should stay
even though I run the other way.

I've lived five days without you
and my soul has found peace,
but my heart still beats anxiously,
waiting for the pain to come again,
like it always does.

I feel deserving
of all the pain you've bestowed upon me.
I feel guilty for wanting to leave,
because the sickest part of me
fears that I don't deserve more.
I worry this is what I must atone for.

Maybe I deserve this, the pain I've endured.
Maybe this is simply how men will treat me.
I fear I might never get the chance to see if I'm wrong,
if my beliefs can be disproved by another.

I fear I've already been ruined, completely.
He has taken parts of my utmost being
and stained them with his insanity.
I deserve this,
I tell myself
as I watch the cuts bleed.

Deeper and deeper they go,
until I cannot feel anymore.
I'm numb to the pain.
At least I tell myself that
after I've cried all the stinging away.

I deserve this.
I deserve the pain I've been through.
I am unclean in every way.
And he dares to tell me,
"It's not my fault, okay?
You just remember things differently."
My tears burn as they escape my eyes
late at night as I cry.

What did I do to deserve the nightmares
and the subsequent years of therapy
that have yet to work?

Maybe I deserve to hurt.

TORTURE

The devil sits behind my back,
Waiting for its next chance to attack.
In a black long-sleeved old tee,
He waits impatiently for my vulnerability.
Then he will feast on my heart as it bleeds
From the knife he carved into me.

YOU SING A SONG OF REDEMPTION
THAT QUIETS MY FEARS

He painted me as the person I never wanted to be.
I looked in the mirror
and didn't recognize the person before me.
The guilt ate me up inside.
My hands have been where they should never be,
and my mind has seen things that I wish to unsee.
My heart had broken apart too many times
for me to count, and he had to agree.
I lived behind a wall of lies, saying everything was fine.
But I was waging a war in solitude, suffocating
on reality, suffering in every sense.
I was listless.
I just wanted to be like the girls I'd seen,
happy,
content, and thriving in their own bodies.
Why can't I be like her?
But I wonder if they have insecurities they don't show.
If they feel like me,
a deep, ever-present need for self-improvement.
There's always something to be fixed,
something we wish we could change,
parts of ourselves we'd slice off or rearrange.

My heart hurts and my mind is tired,
and I've tried so long to pretend to be inspired,
but I'm merely wired on anxiety and self-pity,
loathing who I am entirely.
My hands ache from my past mistakes,
the drywall I hit that left me with a near-break.

I want to take it back again and again,
undo the damage done, but I can't.
My errors seem to be written in the stars,
as if they're my destiny.
Is this all I'm meant to be?
To feel this perpetual ache?
I want to be better,
but my skies are clouded and so is my judgment.
I can't possibly be someone He would want to claim.
My sins are too big, too grievous.
They live within me.
My demons pull at my inseams and tug at my utmost being.
They tell me this is all I was meant to be,
a girl who messes up everything.
No one could ever love a girl like me,
that's what they told me.
They whispered,
It doesn't matter
and neither do you,
so do whatever the hell you want to do.

But I silence those lies with Your truth.
I've been forgiven and even my darkest
and heaviest sins have been removed.
I'm free from the burdens that used to consume me.
My hands have been cleaned,
and my wrongs have been redeemed.
All because of the scars You endured for me.

WHEN DID THESE FOUR WALLS START TO FEEL LIKE A CAGE?

You asked, "What did I do?"

And that's when I realized I couldn't answer you.
Not in the way you wanted me to.

You hadn't done anything.
That was the problem all along.

You never showed interest in my life
or bothered to ask how I was
after a two-hour panic attack
I had in the middle of the night.

You didn't care to know my friends' names
or the reasons why I cried out in pain.
You couldn't be bothered
to ask about me, my life, anything.

But still,
you blamed me
for your lack of presence
in my life.

You said I was going through a phase
that you simply didn't like.
Every kid hates their parents from time to time, you'd say.

But you were wrong.
It wasn't a phase.
And it wasn't my fault.

My favorite color is still a mystery to you.
And I blame you
for all you did
and everything you didn't do.

So when you ask me again,
"What did I do?"
I'll tell you,
"It's all that you didn't do...
all the things you were supposed to."

YOU LOVED TO WATCH ME BLEED

He cut my sides
And severed my tongue
And told me I was the one who stung

THE WORLD DOESN'T REVOLVE AROUND YOU

You always had to turn the conversation
back around to you,
It makes sense;
that's what you liked to talk about most,
you.

I told you I had been sick for a week,
and you said you had just been sick for a month.
It was always a competition,
a contest of suffering,
because you always needed others' pity,
others' admiration,
anything.
You said it like it was supposed to make me feel better,
or perhaps you wanted me to feel sorry for you.
But I didn't,
not now,
not then.

I rolled my eyes at your remark,
knowing I'd never receive a *get well soon*,
only ever comments about you.

You had a talent for making a conversation
all about you.
No matter the situation,
you could always bring it back to you.

Something you did,
someone you met,
some place you'd been.
You needed the public celebration,
the outward validation,
the attention,
the spotlight,
all on you
every godforsaken night.

Everybody's story
somehow wound up becoming a story
about you.
You couldn't listen without thinking
How some scenario also applied to you.

You couldn't praise me without praising yourself too.

Maybe this is why I stopped talking to you;
I could never talk about anything I wanted
without you diverting it back to you.
Even a dumb science question
for my elementary school homework
led to you talking about your days in university.
And all I wanted to know
was how far the sun was from the moon.

But in fifth grade,
I learned that was too complex of a question for you.

I later learned you cheated your way through,
barely passing,
but you talked yourself up on a pedestal,
making yourself seem big,
successful.

The person who claimed to know everything
failed to know even the littlest bit about me.

I was a complete mystery
that he had no intention of solving.

I was a million-dollar Monet
packed away
and rotting in a shed.

He glanced every now and then, admiring my beauty,
dusting off the edges, then leaving again.

So I remained,
slowly decaying,
with no admirers,
no recognition.

But I belonged in a museum,
amongst a sanctuary of beautiful things,
for eyes deserving of me.

You never cared to know the detailed brushstrokes
of my personality or the things
that caused the canvas of my being
to split and tear at the seams.

I was a maze with two right turns
that you didn't even bother entering.
It wasn't worth your time to take two steps forward,
so you took hundreds back,
saying the maze should unwind itself
so it would be easier for you to complete.

You wanted to just stand there and play your part,
pretending you knew the true beauty of my art.

How dare you come to me
and pretend to know me after everything?

You don't even know my dreams,
the things you took away from me.
The reason I cry in my sleep.

You don't know me,
and you never did.
You never wanted to,
not even when I was a kid.

How dare you tell a child
it's their job to grow to appease you
and do everything you never had the ambition to do?

How dare you tell me it was my job to get to know you?
Wasn't your love supposed to be unconditional?

But you blamed me
for your inability
to love me
the way I deserved to be.

You could never take responsibility.
Luckily, I didn't inherit that from my family tree.
And I'm so sorry you never got to know me
and for missing out on all that I grew to be.

Because one day
I'll be recovered
from the ruin of you.

And I'll glow beneath a golden hue
of sunlight and love.

And they'll see me
beyond the lens of you,
no longer through.

Apart from you,
I'm complete.

An evergreen
waiting to be seen
by the people who will truly love me.

THIS ISN'T GOODBYE

Endings aren't always the end.
They don't always mean the story is over.
Sometimes, they are merely the conclusion
of one chapter and the start of a new one.

The first chapter of my story has been told.
My thoughts have been written
and transformed into art.
My heart is so full,
and for the first time in years
there's a good reason for my tears.
I'm so grateful for those
who have fought for me
and believed in me.
And to those who doubted me
and thought my dreams were silly,
I'm here despite your disbelief.
To everyone who ever hurt me,
you've made me who I am today,
but I won't say thank you for the pain.

And after living in many houses,
I've learned the pain of losing a home
and trying to find space for your baggage
in someone else's bedroom.
But your luggage never fits like it did
at your place of origin.
My passion is homegrown
and so is my pain.

So I cling to my mother,
my closest companion,
through everything.
I couldn't have done it without her,
surviving as long as I have,
living after the death of so many things.

Thank you for believing in me
and teaching me that it's okay to leave
people,
places,
and things that no longer serve me.
You've been a life jacket when I was sinking,
and in the depths of my despair,
you've always been there.

This isn't the end of my story,
this is just the beginning.
And I can't wait to watch my story unfold before me,
to witness all its twists and turns,
its highs and lows.
I know God has so much good in store.

I find myself unrelenting with words,
unable to be satisfied with endings,
so I am always writing,
always creating.

Because in a world of overconsumption,
I must create for my own sake;
to quiet the voices in my mind
and slow the passage of time.

My hands cannot rest,
and my verbosity
will always get the better of me.

But for now,
I will be content with this.

Within your hands,
you hold my dream,
you grasp my heart
that's been pulled apart
at the seams.
Don't let anyone convince you
of incapability.
You are full of wonder and possibility
and far more than you think —
at least that's what my mother told me.

Dreams do come true.
They did for me,
and they can for you.

Until next time,
thank you.

I'll see you soon...

ACKNOWLEDGMENTS

For My English Teachers

I'm so grateful for all the English teachers I've had throughout my education who sparked my love of writing. I especially want to thank two of my favorite teachers who believed in me and truly inspired me. I am so thankful for the two of you. It is because of you that I realized I wanted to be a writer.

For Ms. Curtis

Amanda Curtis Abney, my seventh and eighth-grade English teacher (because I was blessed enough to have you two years in a row!), it was your class that first sparked my love of writing. I remember the poetry unit you taught so vividly and the feeling of falling in love with how words could be used to convey emotions in such an artistic way. I remember the poem I wrote that made writing feel like an art form rather than a chore, full of endless possibilities. It was a mediocre poem about the ocean, which was ironic, because at the time, I had only seen the Texas beach and didn't have a clue about the true beauty of a seascape.

I find myself often reminiscing on the poem that made me fall in love with poetry, "Dover Beach," by Matthew Arnold. After reading that poem in your class, I realized I wanted to be a poet. My writer's notebook quickly became a personal journal where I poured my heart out, and I found solace for the first time in my life between pages. The black-and-white composition book became an outlet I desperately needed, and during our free-writing time, I wrote about my life and my father and things I didn't dare to speak about. Before, I had only ever written about mundane happenings, but now it all felt different, as if a switch had been flipped and I had found my divine purpose. Thank you for inspiring me to make this book and pursue my dreams. You always encouraged me and commended my writing. You've had a profound impact on my life, and I am truly and deeply grateful. Thank you for who you are and all that you've done for me.

For Mr. Leeves

Hunter Leeves, my 10th-grade English teacher, thank you for being one of the first men in my life to support my dreams and encourage me. It was your first year of teaching, and your nervousness was palpable, but that didn't stop you from making a lasting impact on me. I remember when you sat me down at the end of the year and told me that I would do amazing in AP English as a junior, and that felt like the biggest gold star I could've received. Alas, because of my anxiety, I didn't enroll in honors, but knowing I was capable felt so reassuring.

You could see all the things I was capable of before I could. I kept the papers you graded where you wrote kind notes. "This was excellent, Lauren. You have a talent. Keep pursuing it," you wrote on my paper about the flawed standards of beauty. You've changed my life by believing in me.

And I remember the day you told my class your age, the same as my brother. I was shocked because you couldn't have been more different than him. You were mature and caring, nothing like my brother, yet in so many ways I imagined you as one, as some sort of mentor and male figure that I never had. You were always there for me, always uplifting me, whether that was through an open door or a listening ear. You'd often let me sit in your classroom during lunch, just to sit in silence as I ate. It was the first time in my life that I experienced depression, and in your room, I had a safe space. I told you about my dad; I opened up to you, and you listened. I remember taking a picture with you on my 16th birthday. It's an image I have to this day, a treasured memory.

Because of you, I began to tell my stories. You made me believe that they were important and worthy of sharing. With every small gesture and "good job!" note on graded papers, your kindness stuck. You've encouraged me to pursue my dreams more than my father ever has, and I'm so thankful for that. Thank you for believing in me and helping me to believe in myself.

For Jeffrey Swan

Jeffrey D. Swan, I don't even know where to begin, so I'll start with thank you. Thank you for truly caring. When I spoke, you didn't just listen — you heard me and empathized with me on a level no man ever had. And I know therapy is your profession, but you always felt more like a friend. When I started seeing you in my senior year of high school, I was a mess. My anxiety and panic attacks were the worst they had been, and you graciously agreed to see me for a reduced rate as my family couldn't afford ongoing therapy for me at the time. I remember the anxiety I felt before I ever walked in and how my stomach twisted in the waiting room. I remember the first time I sat on that couch in your office; I don't think I got a full sentence out before I started crying. Something about you made me feel so comfortable, so vulnerable, like I was able to let all of my emotions pour out freely.

I realize now that something was you and who you are as a person. You are one of the kindest and most tender-hearted people I know. Your empathy was overwhelming, and I felt like, for the first time in my life, someone could see me for me. You could see me right down to my heart and soul. Thank you for giving me a safe space to share my anxiety and trauma, for being someone to cry with me for all that I'd been through, and for assuring me that my pain was valid. Thank you for meeting me again years later to catch up, for reading my poetry, and for encouraging me to share my story. Thank you for telling me that everything I do is done with care, purpose, and loving intention.

Thank you for being you.

ABOUT THE AUTHOR

Lauren Hope Bartling is a writer, poet, and dreamer born, raised, and based in Austin, Texas. She attended Liberty University and graduated in 2020 with a Bachelor of Science in Elementary Education and a minor in Creative Writing.

She fell in love with poetry in middle school, began writing poems at 15 to release the emotions she had been repressing, and hasn't stopped since.

When Lauren is not frantically writing down a new idea for a poem or a plot point for a novel, she can be found reading, listening to Taylor Swift, or spending too much time on social media.